Prepared in cooperation with the Pennsylvania Fish and Boat Commission and the Pennsylvania Department of Environmental Protection

Streamflow and Water-Quality Monitoring in Response to Young-of-Year Smallmouth Bass (*Micropterus dolomieu*) Mortality in the Susquehanna River and Major Tributaries, with Comparisons to the Delaware and Allegheny Rivers, Pennsylvania, 2008–10

Open-File Report 2012–1019

U.S. Department of the Interior
U.S. Geological Survey

Streamflow and Water-Quality Monitoring in Response to Young-of-Year Smallmouth Bass (*Micropterus dolomieu*) Mortality in the Susquehanna River and Major Tributaries, with Comparisons to the Delaware and Allegheny Rivers, Pennsylvania, 2008–10

By Jeffrey J. Chaplin and J. Kent Crawford

Prepared in cooperation with the
Pennsylvania Fish and Boat Commission and
the Pennsylvania Department of Environmental Protection

Open-File Report 2012–1019

U.S. Department of the Interior
U.S. Geological Survey

U.S. Department of the Interior
KEN SALAZAR, Secretary

U.S. Geological Survey
Marcia K. McNutt, Director

U.S. Geological Survey, Reston, Virginia: 2012

For more information on the USGS—the Federal source for science about the Earth, its natural and living resources, natural hazards, and the environment, visit http://www.usgs.gov or call 1–888–ASK–USGS.

For an overview of USGS information products, including maps, imagery, and publications, visit http://www.usgs.gov/pubprod

To order this and other USGS information products, visit http://store.usgs.gov

Suggested citation:
Chaplin, J.J., and Crawford, J.K., 2012, Streamflow and water-quality monitoring in response to young-of-year small-mouth bass (*micropterus dolomieu*) mortality in the Susquehanna River and major tributaries, with comparisons to the Delaware and Allegheny Rivers, Pennsylvania, 2008–10: U.S. Geological Survey Open-File Report 2012–1019, 39 p.

Contents

Figures

Tables

Conversion Factors and Datums

SI to Inch/Pound

Multiply	By	To obtain
Length		
centimeter (cm)	0.3937	inch (in.)
millimeter (mm)	0.03937	inch (in.)
meter (m)	3.281	foot (ft)
kilometer (km)	0.6214	mile (mi)
Area		
square kilometer (km^2)	0.3861	square mile (mi^2)
Volume		
liter (L)	0.2642	gallon (gal)
cubic meter (m^3)	264.2	gallon (gal)
Flow rate		
meter per second (m/s)	3.281	foot per second (ft/s)
cubic meter per second (m^3/s)	35.31	cubic foot per second (ft^3/s)
cubic meter per second (m^3/s)	22.83	million gallons per day (Mgal/d)

Temperature in degrees Celsius (°C) may be converted to degrees Fahrenheit (°F) as follows:

°F=(1.8×°C)+32

Temperature in degrees Fahrenheit (°F) may be converted to degrees Celsius (°C) as follows:

°C=(°F-32)/1.8

Vertical coordinate information is referenced to the North American Vertical Datum of 1988 (NAVD 88).

Horizontal coordinate information is referenced to the North American Datum of 1983 (NAD 83) unless otherwise noted.

Altitude, as used in this report, refers to distance above the vertical datum.

*Transmissivity: The standard unit for transmissivity is cubic foot per day per square foot times foot of aquifer thickness [(ft^3/d)/ft^2]ft. In this report, the mathematically reduced form, foot squared per day (ft^2/d), is used for convenience.

Specific conductance is given in microsiemens per centimeter at 25 degrees Celsius (μS/cm at 25°C).

Concentrations of chemical constituents in water are given in either milligrams per liter (mg/L) or micrograms per liter (μg/L).

A water year is the period extending from October 1 through September 30. It is designated by the calendar year in which it ends.

(This page intentionally left blank.)

Streamflow and Water-Quality Monitoring in Response to Young-of-Year Smallmouth Bass (*Micropterus dolomieu*) Mortality in the Susquehanna River and Major Tributaries, with Comparisons to the Delaware and Allegheny Rivers, Pennsylvania, 2008–10

Abstract

Since 2005, spring hatched young-of-year (YOY) small-mouth bass in Pennsylvania reaches of the Susquehanna River have experienced above-normal mortality when summertime streamflows are near or lower than normal. Stress factors include, but are not limited to, low dissolved oxygen and elevated water temperatures during times critical for survival and development (critical period is May 1 through July 31). At this time (2010), widespread disease and mortality are believed to be more prevalent for YOY smallmouth bass in the Susquehanna River Basin than in the Delaware or Allegheny River Basins.

The U.S. Geological Survey began a study in 2008 to investigate water temperature and dissolved oxygen as possible stressors to the YOY smallmouth bass. Monitoring began in 2008 and continued in 2009 and 2010 in selected reaches. Continuous (30-minute intervals) measurements of dissolved oxygen, water temperature, pH, and specific conductance were made during all or parts of the study at stations including, but not limited to, the Delaware River at Trenton, N.J. (station C1), Susquehanna River at Clemson Island (station C4), Juniata River at Newport, Pa. (station C5), Juniata River at Howe Township Park (station C6), Susquehanna River at Harrisburg, Pa. (station C8), and Allegheny River at Acmetonia, Pa. (station C10). At stations C1, C5, and C8, streamflow data also were collected. Streamflow data were not collected at stations C4, C6, and C10; therefore, data from nearby streamgages on the Susquehanna River at Sunbury, Pa. (station N8), the Juniata River at Newport, Pa (station C5), and the Allegheny River at Natrona, Pa. (station C9), were used to represent flow conditions at these stations.

Streamflow during the critical period of each year influenced dissolved-oxygen concentrations and water temperature, and was associated with the incidence of disease in YOY smallmouth bass. During the critical period of 2009, station C8 had a median daily streamflow of 26,300 cubic feet per second (ft³/s), approximately two times higher than for the critical periods in 2008 and 2010. Diseased YOY smallmouth bass were captured at only 3 sites in 2009 but 19 sites in 2008 and 28 sites in 2010.

During relatively low streamflow in the critical periods of 2008 and 2010, dissolved-oxygen concentrations also were lower (more stressful to aquatic life) than in 2009. During the critical period, median daily minimum dissolved-oxygen concentrations in main-channel habitat of the Susquehanna River at station C8 were lower in 2008 and 2010 by 1.2 milligrams per liter (mg/L) and 1.5 mg/L, respectively, in comparison to the median daily minimum concentrations in 2009. Despite the year-to-year differences in dissolved oxygen, results of a comparison of data for station C8 from each year of the study period with historical data from 1974–79 indicate daily minimum dissolved-oxygen concentrations in all 3 years of the study were significantly lower than those from the historical dataset (p-values less than 0.05). Although lower streamflows for critical periods of 2008–10 may help explain statistical differences in dissolved oxygen between the two time periods, other factors such as long-term streamwater warming trends also may play a role.

Median daily minimum dissolved-oxygen concentration in the microhabitat of the Susquehanna River at Clemson Island (station C4) was 1.6 mg/L lower in 2008 than 2009. No data were collected at station C4 in 2010. For the microhabitat of the Juniata River near Howe Township Park (station C6), median daily minimum dissolved-oxygen concentrations were about 0.6 mg/L lower in 2008 than in 2010. At station C6, no data were collected in 2009.

Nighttime concentrations of dissolved oxygen in micro-habitats at stations C4 and C6 were at times lower than the 5.0-mg/L criterion established by the U.S. Environmental Protection Agency for early life stages of warm-water fish. The most frequent occurrence of dissolved oxygen less than 5.0 mg/L was at station C4 (31 of 92 days in the critical period of 2008). The longest duration that dissolved oxygen was lower than 5.0 mg/L was 8.5 hours (station C4; 23:30 on June 10, 2008, to 08:00 on June 11, 2008).

Median daily maximum water temperatures in the main channel of the Susquehanna River at station C8 were 4.0 degrees Celsius (°C) higher in 2008 and 4.3°C warmer in 2010 than in 2009 during the critical periods. At station C8, the water temperatures during the critical periods of all 3 years were significantly warmer (p-values <0.05) than during the critical periods of 1974–79. Year-to-year water-temperature differences in the main-channel habitat of the Juniata River at station C5 were slightly less than year-to-year differences in the Susquehanna River at station C8. During the critical periods, the water temperature at station C5 was 3.5°C warmer in 2008 and 3.3°C warmer in 2010 than in 2009. These results are consistent with warming trends documented in other streams of the northeastern United States with much more robust water-temperature datasets.

For the critical period of each year, dissolved oxygen in the Susquehanna River at station C8 typically was 1.5 to 3.0 mg/L lower than in the Delaware River at station C1 and the Allegheny River at station C10. Median daily maximum water temperatures during the critical period of each year ranged from 1.6 to 2.7°C warmer at station C8 than at stations C1 and C10.

Introduction

The smallmouth bass (*Micropterus dolomieu*) is native to the Great Lakes and Ohio River watersheds but was introduced throughout the United States in the second half of the 19th century (Pennsylvania Fish and Boat Commission, 2009). Today, major drainages to the Chesapeake Bay, including the Potomac and Shenandoah Rivers in Maryland, West Virginia, and Virginia and the Susquehanna River in New York, Pennsylvania, and Maryland, are widely recognized as high-quality smallmouth-bass fisheries with historically strong recruitment. Great public concern over the viability of smallmouth bass and other fish species living in these rivers began in the summer of 2002, when extensive die-offs of primarily adult fish (including smallmouth bass) were documented in the West Virginia part of the South Branch Potomac River (Garman and Orth, 2007). From 2004 to 2006, additional fish kills occurred in the Shenandoah River Basin in Virginia, with 80 percent mortality of adult smallmouth bass and redbreast sunfish along 100 miles of the South Fork Shenandoah River in 2005 (Ripley and others, 2008).

In reaches of the Susquehanna River within Pennsylvania, dead and moribund (nearly dead) young-of-year (YOY) smallmouth bass (those hatched in the spring of a given calendar year) were found in quantities greater than background levels in the summer of 2005. Since 2005, mortality has been widespread in years with near-normal or low streamflow. The dead and dying YOY smallmouth bass have had internal and external bacterial infections (Pennsylvania Fish and Boat Commission, 2005; Vicki Blazer, U.S. Geological Survey, written commun., 2010). The external infections are characterized by white skin lesions (fig. 1).

Environmental stressors that may predispose fish to colonization by bacteria and other pathogens include, but are not limited to, low dissolved-oxygen, elevated ammonia, and elevated nitrite concentrations, and warm water temperatures

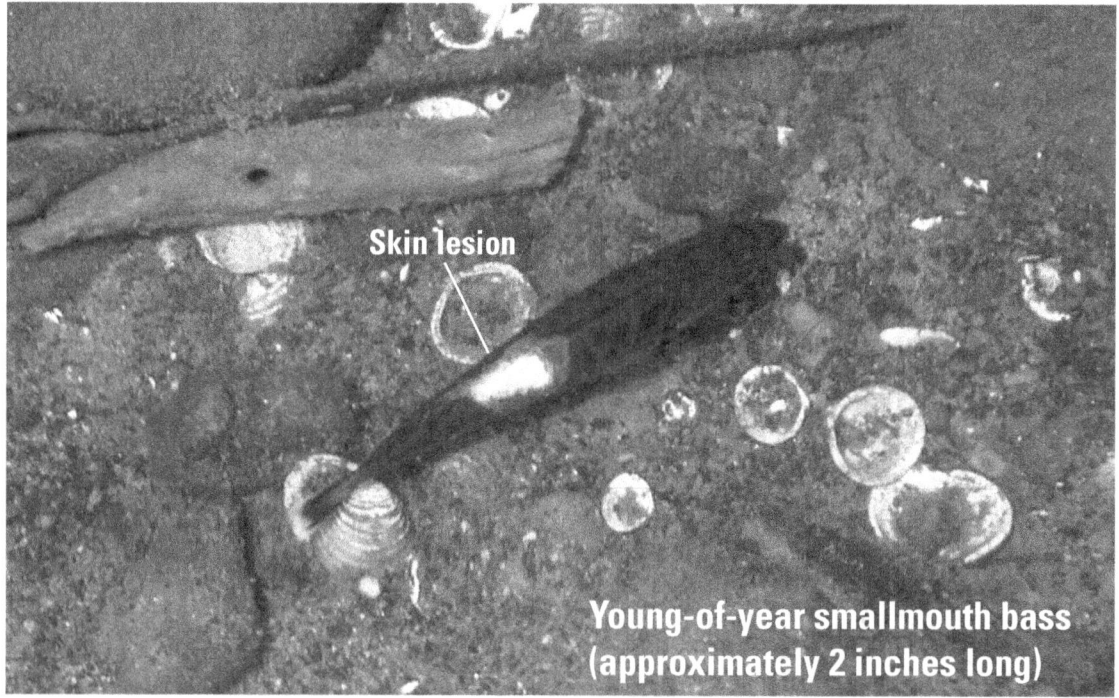

Figure 1.   Young-of-year smallmouth bass (*Micropterus dolomieu*) with a skin lesion swimming in the Susquehanna River near Mahantango, Pa. Photograph by Joseph Cukjati, U.S. Geological Survey, July 12, 2010.

(Durborow and others, 1998). Low dissolved oxygen and (or) elevated water temperatures, along with other environmental stressors, have the potential to cause a physiological stress response, resulting in altered circulating concentrations of the hormone cortisol (Ripley and others, 2008). Immunosuppression from increased cortisol concentrations can cause reductions in circulating immune cell numbers and bactericidal activity coinciding with an inflammatory response (Maule and Schreck, 1990; Wang and others, 2005). Reconnaissance water-quality sampling by Pennsylvania Fish and Boat Commission (PFBC) biologists in 2007 indicated nighttime concentrations of dissolved oxygen in the Susquehanna River near Sunbury, Pa., were sometimes less than 5.0 milligrams per liter (mg/L), which is the recommended national criterion for protecting early life stages of warm-water fish (U.S. Environmental Protection Agency, 1986). As a result, the U.S. Geological Survey (USGS) began investigating dissolved oxygen and water temperature as possible stressors. The solubility of oxygen in equilibrium with water and air is inversely related to water temperature and atmospheric pressure; however, in summertime and early fall, equilibrium conditions rarely are achieved because of photosynthesis and respiration. During the day, the rate of oxygen production by photosynthesis exceeds the rate at which oxygen exsolves into the atmosphere. As a result, the water becomes supersaturated with oxygen despite relatively high daytime water temperatures. In contrast, cooler nighttime water temperature generally results in lower dissolved-oxygen concentrations because respiration consumes oxygen in the water faster than it dissolves into the water column.

In 2008, low dissolved-oxygen concentrations (less than 5.0 mg/L) were measured primarily in habitat characterized by relatively shallow, slow-moving water in nearshore areas (Chaplin and others, 2009). These areas are inhabited by YOY smallmouth bass for the first few months of life and are referred to as "YOY smallmouth bass microhabitats" in this report. In most Pennsylvania rivers, summertime dissolved-oxygen concentrations and water temperatures typically follow a diurnal pattern characterized by daily minima in the early morning hours (between 0300 and 0700) and daily maxima in late afternoon (between 1400 and 1800) (fig. 2). In 2008, concentrations of dissolved oxygen less than 5.0 mg/L were documented during the expected timeframe (nighttime to early morning hours; Chaplin and others, 2009) in the Susquehanna River between Sunbury, Pa., and Harrisburg, Pa., and in the Juniata River downstream from Newport, Pa. (fig. 3).

Since continuous monitoring of dissolved oxygen, water temperature, and other characteristics was initiated in 2008, the PFBC, USGS, and Pennsylvania Department of Environmental Protection (PADEP) have collaborated on a variety of other investigations in the Susquehanna River, Juniata River, and selected tributaries (fig. 4). These investigations have included annual population surveys of YOY smallmouth bass by PFBC; health assessments of YOY and adult smallmouth bass by USGS, PFBC, and PADEP; assessment of bacterial and viral infection in YOY and adult smallmouth by USGS;

and measurement of contaminants in water using passive samplers by USGS and PFBC. Although many results are still pending, these research efforts have revealed that the causes of a declining smallmouth bass population and disease in YOY are complicated and cannot be explained by one environmental stressor or pathogen.

Despite the complicated nature of disease in YOY smallmouth bass, some associations with streamflow and water-quality characteristics are apparent. Streamflow and disease records indicate the incidence of disease was widespread in summers with near-normal or low streamflow and relatively high water temperature (Chaplin and others, 2009). When water temperature is relatively warm, dissolved-oxygen concentrations can be depressed, leading to a stressed aquatic environment that does not directly cause disease in YOY smallmouth bass, but can modify the role of pathogens, contaminants, or other factors more directly linked to a cause.

Continuous data for streamflow, dissolved oxygen, and water temperature, along with other characteristics including pH and specific conductance, provide an important context for interpreting the role of pathogens, contaminants, or other causes of disease. Recognizing the need for additional study beyond 2008, the USGS, in cooperation with PFBC and PADEP, continued to monitor streamflow and water-quality characteristics in 2009 and 2010 in selected reaches of the Susquehanna River and major tributaries. This study focused on water-quality characteristics in 2009 and 2010, which were then compared with water-quality characteristics in 2008, which are documented by Chaplin and others (2009).

Purpose and Scope

This report presents results and analysis of water-quality data collected from sondes measuring dissolved oxygen, water temperature, pH, and specific conductance continuously (30-minute intervals) from May 1 through July 31 of 2008, 2009, and 2010 (study period). It also provides streamflow data for all or parts of the study period at the following stations: the Susquehanna River at Harrisburg, Pa. (station C8); Juniata River at Newport, Pa. (station C5); Susquehanna River at Sunbury, Pa. (station N8); Delaware River at Trenton, N.J. (station C1); and the Allegheny River at Natrona, Pa. (station C9).

Water-quality data for main-channel habitat in the Susquehanna River, Juniata River, Delaware River, and Allegheny River from 2009 and 2010 are compared with data from 2008. Water-quality data initially collected in 2008 at microhabitats in the Susquehanna River at Clemson Island (station C4) and the Juniata River near Howe Township Park (station C6) are compared with data available for these stations during the same periods of 2009 (station C4 only) and 2010 (station C6 only). For the Susquehanna River at station C8, statistical tests were used to compare historical (1974–79) streamflow and water-quality characteristics with data collected throughout the study period.

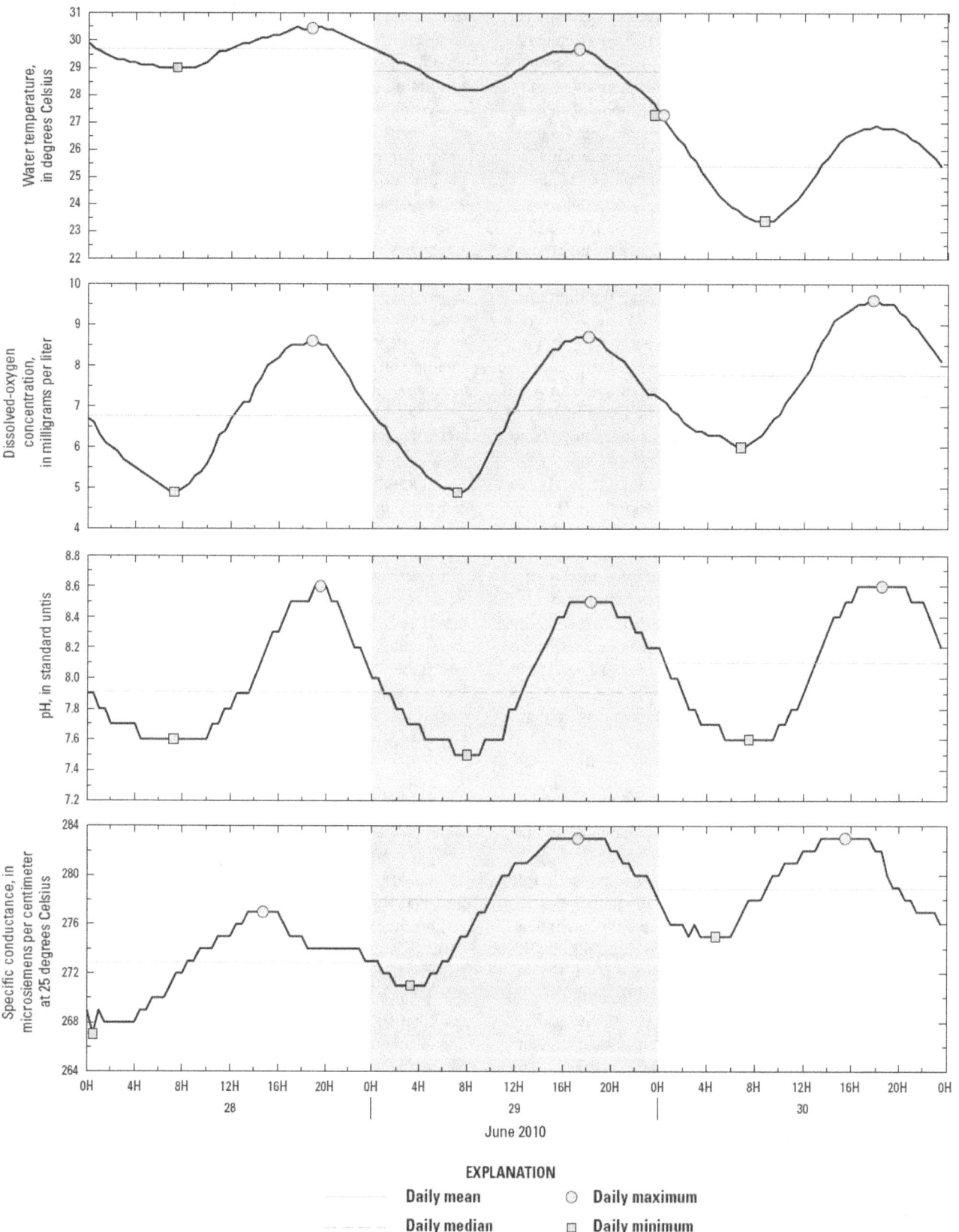

EXPLANATION

| | Daily mean | ○ | Daily maximum |
| | Daily median | □ | Daily minimum |

Figure 2.   Example of typical diurnal fluctuations and associated daily values for water temperature, dissolved oxygen, pH, and specific conductance measured in the Susquehanna River at Harrisburg, Pa. (station C8), June 28–30, 2010.

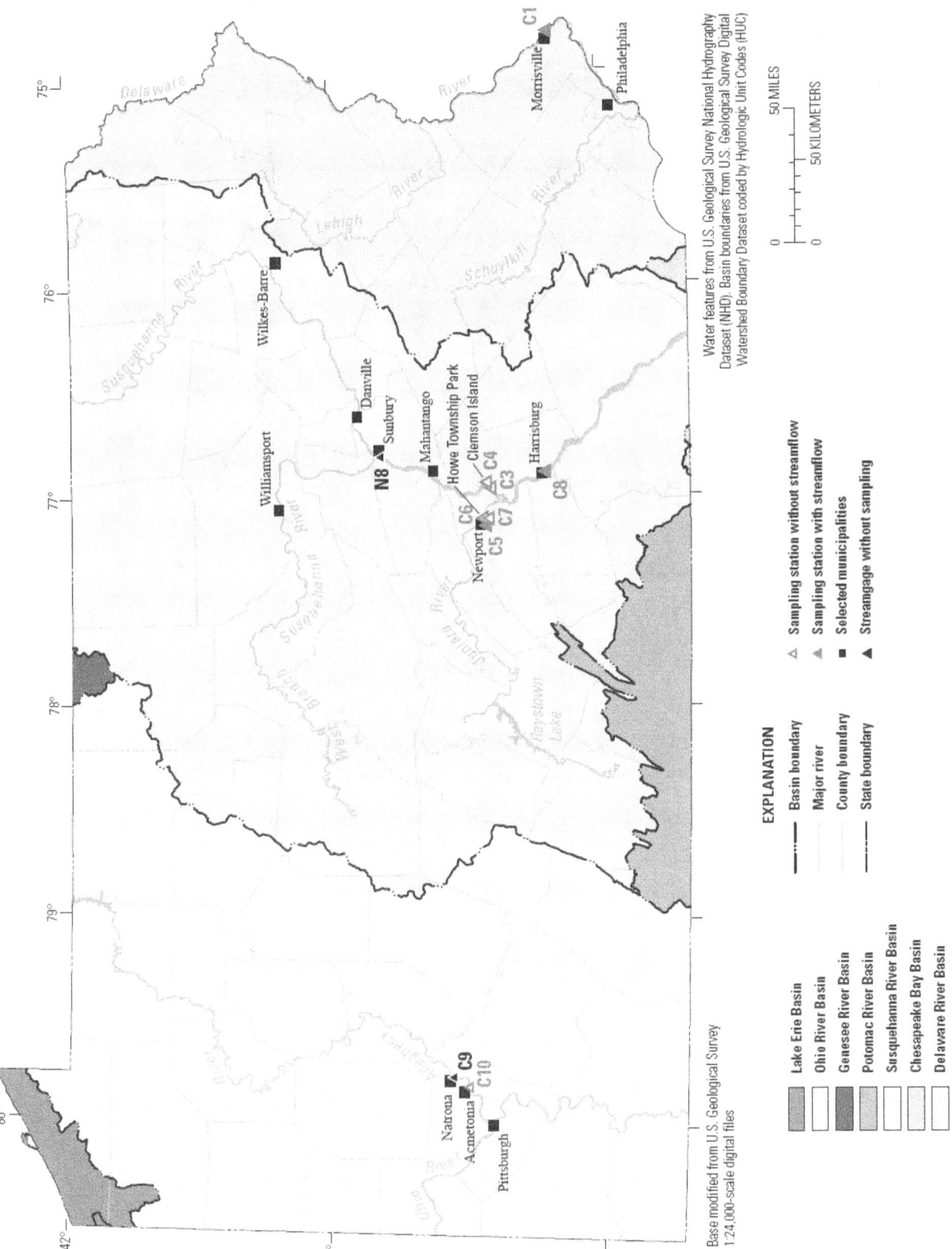

Base modified from U.S. Geological Survey
1:24,000-scale digital files

Water features from U.S. Geological Survey National Hydrography
Dataset (NHD). Basin boundaries from U.S. Geological Survey Digital
Watershed Boundary Dataset coded by Hydrologic Unit Codes (HUC)

EXPLANATION

----- Basin boundary	△ Sampling station without streamflow
——— Major river	▲ Sampling station with streamflow
——— County boundary	■ Selected municipalities
——— State boundary	▲ Streamgage without sampling

Lake Erie Basin
Ohio River Basin
Genesee River Basin
Potomac River Basin
Susquehanna River Basin
Chesapeake Bay Basin
Delaware River Basin

Figure 3. Location of selected continuous water-quality and streamgages in the Delaware, Susquehanna, and Ohio River Basins, Pa., 2008–10. (Selected municipalities are shown to orient the reader.)

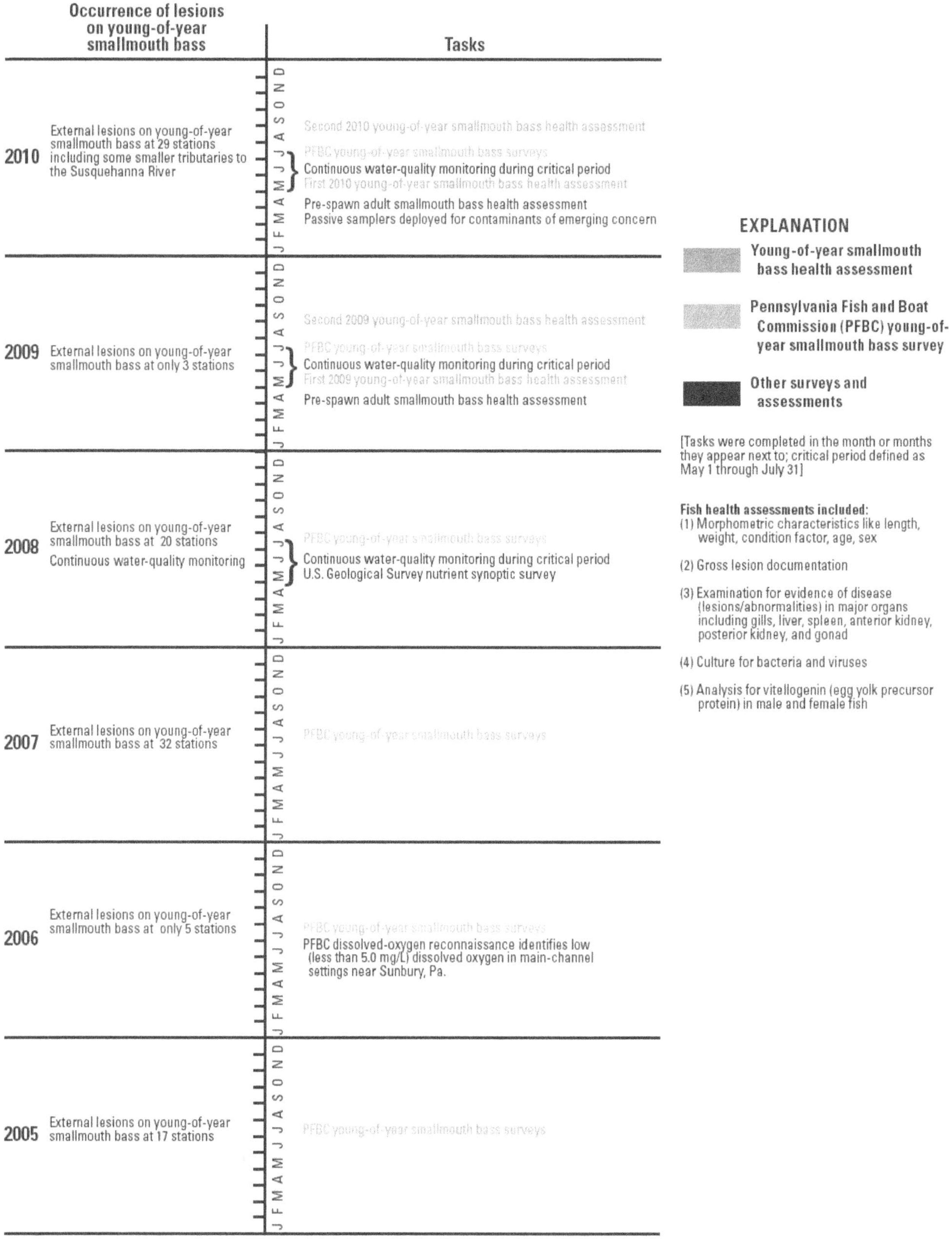

Figure 4.   Selected tasks undertaken by agencies studying young-of-year smallmouth bass mortalities in the Susquehanna River Basin, Pa.

History of Mortality in Young-of-Year Smallmouth Bass, 2005–07

PFBC has conducted annual surveys of YOY smallmouth bass throughout Pennsylvania since the 1980s. Dead and dying YOY smallmouth bass were first documented in Pennsylvania in July 2005, when surveys by PFBC found YOY with skin lesions in the Susquehanna River, West Branch Susquehanna River, and Juniata River. The lesions were not found on adult fish as in the Shenandoah and Potomac Rivers. No fish kills and no lesions on YOY smallmouth bass were documented between 2005 and 2007 or reported by fishermen in other large rivers of Pennsylvania, such as the Delaware or Allegheny (fig. 5). The lesions and associated mortalities were initially thought to be caused solely from infection by *Flavobacterium columnare* (Pennsylvania Fish and Boat Commission, 2005; Chaplin and others, 2009); however, additional bacteria, including *Aeromonas spp.*, are now known to also infect the fish (Vicki Blazer, U.S. Geological Survey, written commun., 2010). In addition to skin lesions, infection by bacteria is often accompanied by gill necrosis and fin rot, all occurring in varying degrees of severity (Decostere and others, 1999). These conditions were widely reported by PFBC biologists and anglers in July 2005. Fish with these symptoms are described as diseased throughout this report; however, it is beyond the scope of this study to differentiate among the various pathogens and diseases responsible for the symptoms.

After discovering diseased YOY smallmouth bass in 2005, PFBC biologists continued to document the presence or absence of disease during subsequent annual summertime population surveys at sampling sites across Pennsylvania (fig. 5). In 2006, which had relatively high spring and summer streamflows (fig. 6), few diseased YOY smallmouth bass were observed in the reaches studied, including reaches where diseased fish had first been discovered in 2005. After the 2006 sampling season, it was unknown whether the disease in 2005 was a one-time event or could be an ongoing problem likely to recur. It also was unknown whether relatively high streamflows in 2006 (compared to 2005) prevented the disease occurrence.

In 2007, summertime streamflows were similar to streamflows in 2005. Diseased fish were again observed in the Susquehanna River Basin but were absent during sampling of the Delaware and Allegheny River Basins. In the summer of 2007, results from water-quality testing by PFBC biologists indicated nighttime concentrations of dissolved oxygen were sometimes stressful (less than 5.0 mg/L). These findings provided the impetus for beginning a water-quality monitoring program in 2008.

Study Design

The study was designed to compare water-quality characteristics at seven stations from May 1 to July 31, defined here as the critical period for the survival and development of YOY smallmouth bass, in 2008, 2009, and 2010. Sondes were first deployed during the critical period in 2008 to continuously measure dissolved oxygen, water temperature, pH, and specific conductance in main-channel habitats and microhabitats (Chaplin and others, 2009). The 2008 effort represented the beginning of long-term monitoring needed to understand water-quality characteristics associated with disease in YOY smallmouth bass. Similar monitoring was conducted in 2009 and 2010. Data from two sondes already operating in the Delaware River at station C1 and the Allegheny River at station C10 were used in all 3 years for comparison to Susquehanna River data to provide insight about why diseased fish were more prevalent in the Susquehanna River than in the Delaware or Allegheny River.

In 2008, four sondes were deployed in pairs to evaluate differences between main-channel habitats and YOY smallmouth bass microhabitats of the Susquehanna River in the vicinity of Clemson Island and the Juniata River near Howe Township Park (table 1; fig. 3). These paired sondes are differentiated as "main-channel" (Susquehanna River below Clemson Island at station C3 and Juniata River near Howe Township Park at station C7) and "microhabitat" (Susquehanna River at station C4 and Juniata River at station C6) throughout this report. Two additional sondes were collocated with streamgages at stations C8 and C5 to represent main-channel habitats of the Susquehanna River at Harrisburg, Pa., and Juniata River at Newport, Pa., respectively. In 2009, sondes were redeployed at all the same stations as in 2008 except stations C6 and C7 in the Juniata River near Howe Township Park. Stations C6 and C7 were eliminated in favor of monitoring microhabitat and main-channel habitat in the Susquehanna River near Clemson Island (stations C3 and C4). In 2010, sondes were deployed in main-channel habitats at stations C8 and C5 only.

Methods

Sondes were serviced every 1 to 2 weeks following guidelines established by Wagner and others (2006). For servicing, freshly calibrated field water-quality meters were positioned with the deployed sonde to collect side-by-side measurements of water temperature, dissolved oxygen, pH, and specific conductance. The deployed sonde was removed, cleaned, and returned to the water. A second set of side-by-side readings was then recorded to determine whether any corrections were necessary as a result of fouling of probes. Following the checks against the field water-quality meter, the deployed sonde was again removed from the water, and data stored in it were downloaded to a field data logger. The calibration of each probe was then checked against calibration standards to determine the drift correction. If the probe exceeded the calibration criteria from Wagner and others (2006), the sondes were recalibrated. The stored data from

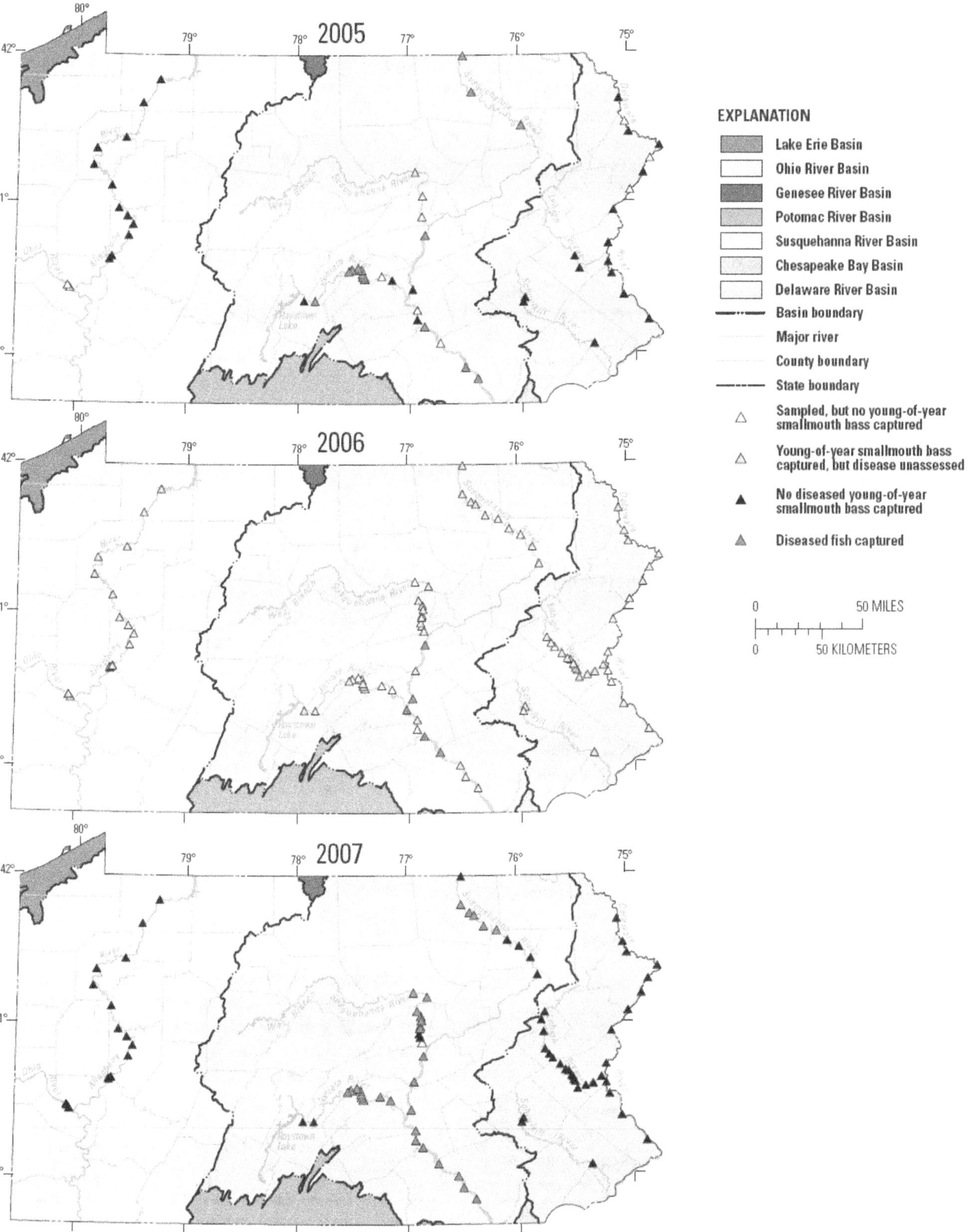

Figure 5.   Geographic distribution of disease incidence in young-of-year smallmouth bass, Pennsylvania, 2005–07. (Data presented on maps for years 2005–07 differ slightly from those presented on similar maps in Chaplin and others (2009) because of new information provided through written and oral communications from Geoffrey Smith, Pennsylvania Fish and Boat Commission, 2010)

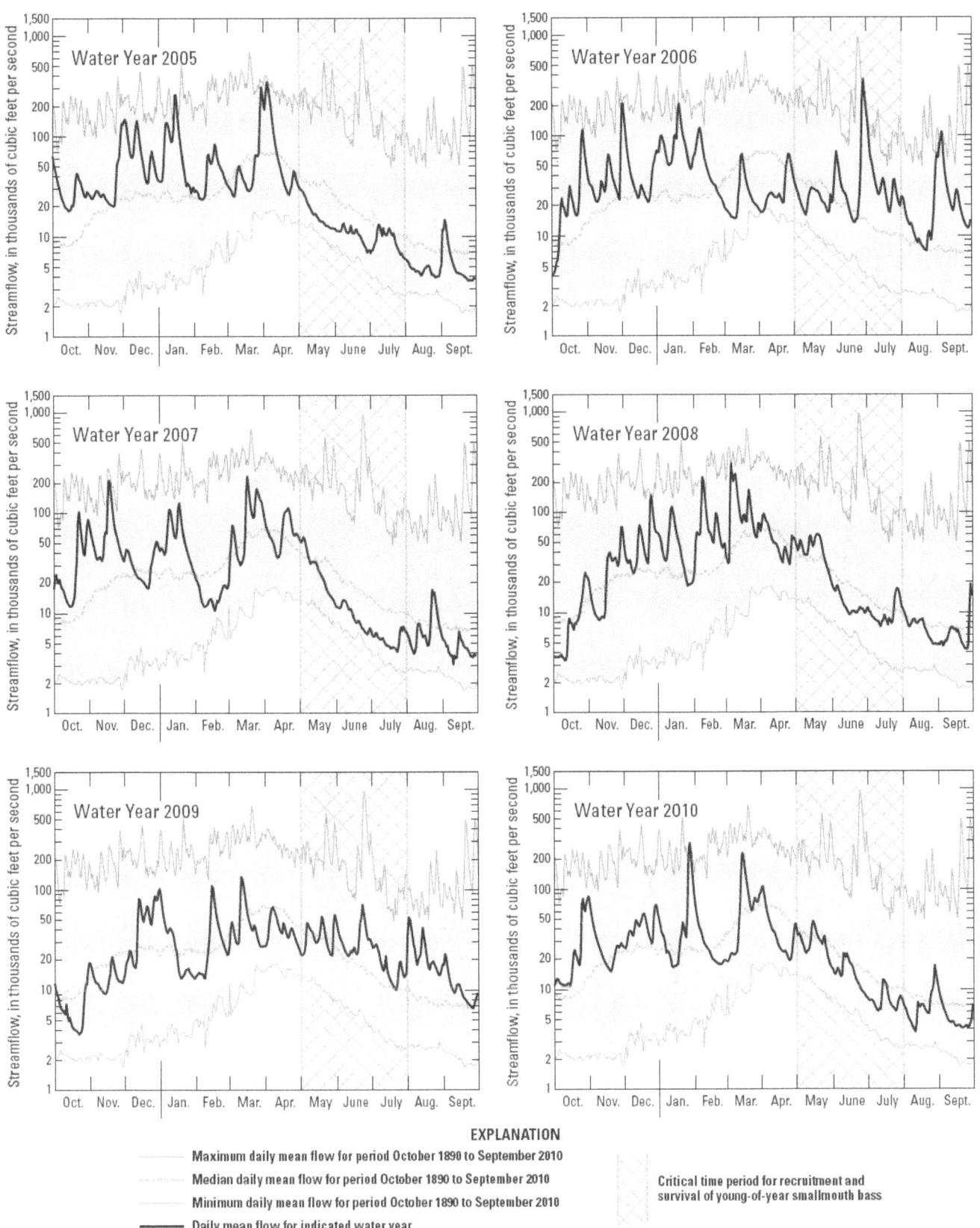

Figure 6. Streamflow in the Susquehanna River at Harrisburg, Pa. (station C8), during water years 2005, 2006, 2007, 2008, 2009, and 2010 compared to the range of streamflows for the entire period of record (1890–2010).

Table 1. Stations used for collection of streamflow and continuous water-quality data, Pennsylvania, 2008–10.

[Horizontal coordinate information is referenced to the North American Datum of 1983 (NAD 83) unless otherwise noted; QW, water quality; mi², square miles; Twp., Township; SF, streamflow; --, not available]

Station number	Map identifier	Station description	Drainage area (mi²)	Period of QW record, calendar year 2008	Period of QW record, calendar year 2009	Period of QW record, calendar year 2010	Latitude	Longitude
01463500	C1	Delaware River at Trenton, N.J.	6,780	01-01 to 12-27	01-02 to 12-31	01-01 to 07-31	40° 13' 18.0"	74° 46' 41.0"
¹01554000	N8	Susquehanna River at Sunbury, Pa.	18,300	SF only	SF only	SF only	²40° 50' 04.0"	²74° 46' 41.0"
01555710	C3	Susquehanna River below Clemson Island, Pa. (Main Channel)	19,673	05-16 to 09-25	05-06 to 10-01	--	40° 27' 42.1"	76° 49' 37.0"
01555725	C4	Susquehanna River at Clemson Island, Pa. (Microhabitat)	19,674	05-16 to 09-25	05-06 to 10-01	--	40° 27' 47.8"	76° 56' 46.3"
01567000	C5	Juniata River at Newport, Pa. (Main Channel)	3,354	05-08 to 10-15	04-24 to 10-02	05-07 to 07-31	²40° 28' 42.0"	²77° 07' 46.0"
01567150	C6	Juniata River near Howe Twp. Park (Microhabitat)	3,379	05-23 to 09-29	--	05-05 to 07-31	40° 29' 29.2"	77° 05' 52.5"
01567151	C7	Juniata River near Howe Twp. Park (Main Channel)	3,379	06-04 to 10-15	--	--	40° 29' 28.2"	77° 05' 50.8"
01570500	C8	Susquehanna River at Harrisburg, Pa. (Main Channel)	24,100	05-15 to 10-10	04-24 to 10-02	05-08 to 07-31	²40° 15' 17.0"	²76° 53' 11.0"
03049500	C9	Allegheny River at Natrona, Pa.	11,410	SF only	SF only	SF only	²40° 32' 10.0"	²79° 43' 07.0"
03049640	C10	Allegheny River at Lock and Dam 3 at Acmetonia, Pa.	11,592	01-01 to 12-30	01-01 to 12-30	01-01 to 07-31	²40° 32' 10.0"	²79° 48' 54.0"

¹Map identifier is "N8" to maintain consistency with the naming convention in Chaplin and others (2009).

²Horizontal coordinate information is referenced to the North American Datum of 1927 (NAD 27).

the deployed sondes were corrected for any fouling or drift, following recommendations of Wagner and others (2006). The adjustments were made using the USGS computer program Automated Data Processing System (ADAPS) (U.S. Geological Survey, 2003). After all adjustments were made for each water-quality characteristic, the records were peer-reviewed, rated, and approved, following methods described in Wagner and others (2006).

ADAPS also was used to store the water-quality data collected every 30 minutes and to compute daily values for each of the characteristics. Examples of daily values include the daily minimum, daily median, daily maximum, and daily mean of water temperature, dissolved oxygen, pH, and specific conductance (fig. 2). These daily values are used throughout this report to summarize the data and for statistical comparisons at station C8. For statistical comparisons, historical daily values during 1974–79 (historical dataset) are compared with (1) data for individual datasets collected in 2008, 2009, and 2010 and (2) median daily values that result from combining the 3 years of data. A two-sided Wilcoxon signed-rank test (Helsel and Hirsch, 2002) was used to test for significant differences at station C8 in streamflow, dissolved oxygen, and water temperature between data collected during the study period and the historical dataset. The pH data were excluded from the tests because there were too few daily values. The null hypothesis for the statistical tests is that there is no difference between data collected during the study period and the historical dataset. For this study, a significant difference exists (the null hypothesis is rejected) if the p-value (probability that a difference occurs by chance) is less than 0.05.

For the statistical comparisons, only data that were available for common days in the historical dataset and the study period (May through July of 2008, 2009, and 2010) were used. For example, if the daily mean water temperature was available for May 10 of 1974, 1975, 1976, 1977, 1978, 1979, and 2008, then this value was included in the comparison. If the value for May 10 was missing in any of those years, then the value was excluded from the analyses. Because some daily values for water temperature and other characteristics are missing in any given year, especially for the historical dataset, the number of observations used in the analyses ranges from 19 (dissolved oxygen) to 92 (streamflow). In general, the power of the statistical tests increases with the number of observations.

Quality Assurance

Protocols for calibrating, deploying, and servicing the continuous-monitoring water-quality meters were derived from the manufacturer's instruction manual (Yellow Springs Instruments, 1999; Wilde and others, 1998; Wagner and others, 2006). Log books for recording calibration, performance, and service information were prepared for each field instrument. Information in these log books was updated during each service visit for each instrument. Log-book records

were used to document calibration accuracies and to track the performance of each instrument over the course of the project. Comprehensive field data sheets were used to record field observations and to ensure that all necessary field observations were completed.

Quality Control

Several quality-control measures were adhered to during the project. Prior to the sampling season, thermistors for field instruments were checked for accuracy against a National Institute for Standards and Technology (NIST) certified thermometer. Instruments for other field measurements (pH, specific conductance, and dissolved oxygen) were calibrated on the day of sampling. Only certified standards and buffers were used for calibrations. Buffers and standards were discarded if the expiration date had passed. One-point dissolved-oxygen calibrations were made using the air-saturation approach (Yellow Springs Instruments, 1999). Readings were adjusted for atmospheric pressure using a Thommen® pocket barometer that had been adjusted to National Weather Service readings and adjusted for the elevation at Harrisburg, Pa. A zero dissolved oxygen solution of sodium sulfite and cobalt chloride, freshly prepared on the days it was needed, was used to check that the dissolved-oxygen meters were accurate at the low end of the range of expected dissolved-oxygen concentrations. Any meter that did not return a dissolved-oxygen reading of 0.3 mg/L or less in a zero dissolved oxygen solution was not used.

Streamflow and Water Quality in the Susquehanna River Basin in 2008, 2009, and 2010

In this section, streamflow and water-quality characteristics measured at selected stations in the Susquehanna River in 2009 and 2010 are compared with results from 2008 (Chaplin and others, 2009) but selected data prior to 2008 are used to provide additional context. Since 2005, when streamflow and disease prevalence data first became available, near-normal or lower streamflows during the critical period [with medians from 9,600 ft^3/s (2007) to 14,300 ft^3/s (2010)] have been associated with relatively high incidence of disease (fig. 7). Critical periods with higher median streamflows, like those in 2006 (26,100 ft^3/s) and 2009 (26,300 ft^3/s), have been associated with lower incidence of disease.

During the study period, diseased YOY smallmouth bass in the Susquehanna River Basin were captured by PFBC at 19 stations in 2008 (median streamflow of 13,100 ft^3/s) and 28 stations in 2010 but only 3 stations in 2009 (figs. 7 and 8). For the critical period of 2006, which was characterized by a median streamflow similar to that of the critical period of 2009, only five stations had diseased YOY smallmouth bass.

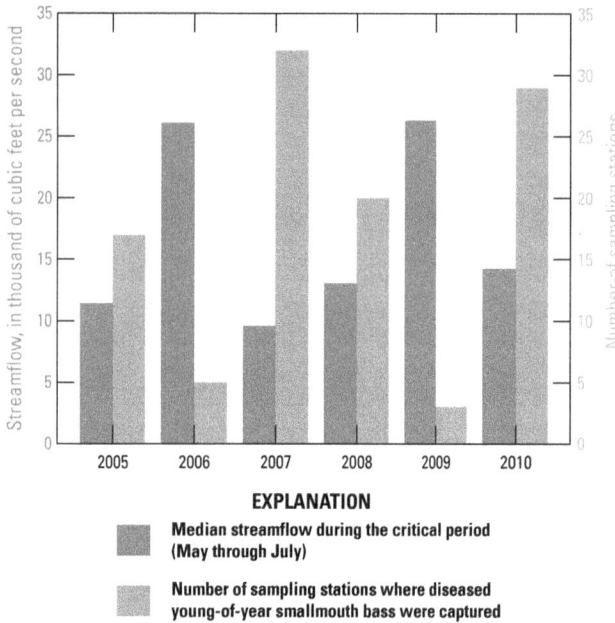

Figure 7.   Median daily streamflow in the Susquehanna River at Harrisburg, Pa. (station C8), during the critical period (May through July) and the number of stations with diseased young-of-year (YOY) smallmouth bass, Pennsylvania, 2005–10.

Annual YOY smallmouth bass collections were expanded by PFBC in 2010 to include 10 additional tributaries to the Susquehanna River within Pennsylvania. Bacterial infections resulting in lesions were documented in 7 of the 10 previously unassessed tributaries. These were the first records of the disease condition in smaller, warm-water streams within the Susquehanna River Basin.

During relatively low streamflow in 2008 and 2010, water-quality characteristics were appreciably different from those in 2009, when fewer diseased YOY were observed (fig. 8). In main-channel habitats at stations C8 and C5, dissolved-oxygen concentrations during the critical period presented more stressful conditions for YOY in 2008 and 2010 than in 2009. During the critical periods of 2008 and 2010, median daily minimum dissolved-oxygen concentrations in the Susquehanna River at station C8 were 1.2 mg/L and 1.5 mg/L, respectively, lower than in 2009 (fig. 9A, B, and C; tables 1–1, 1–2, and 1–3). Differences in median daily minimum dissolved-oxygen concentrations were similar at station C5, with concentrations in 2008 and 2010 being 1.5 mg/L, 1.1 mg/L lower than in 2009 (fig. 10A, B, and C; tables 1–1, 1–2, and 1–3).

YOY smallmouth bass microhabitats generally have lower dissolved-oxygen concentrations than nearby main-channel habitats (Chaplin and others, 2009). In this report, few comparisons can be made for microhabitats because water-quality data were not collected over all 3 years of the

study period. Nonetheless, data that are available indicate the microhabitat setting in the Susquehanna River at station C4 had daily minimum dissolved-oxygen concentrations that were about 1.6 mg/L lower during the critical period of 2008 than in the same timeframe in 2009 (fig. 11A and B). No data were collected at station C4 in 2010. For the Juniata River at station C6, dissolved-oxygen concentrations were about 0.6 mg/L lower in 2008 than in 2010; (fig. 12A and B). No comparison with 2009 can be made at station C6 because no water-quality data were collected in 2009.

In microhabitat of the Susquehanna River at station C4, daily minimum dissolved-oxygen concentrations in 2008 were lower than 5.0 mg/L for periods lasting up to 8.5 hours on 31 days during the critical period (fig. 11A). In contrast, dissolved oxygen at station C4 was at or lower than the 5.0-mg/L criterion on only 2 days during the critical period in 2009 (fig. 11B). For the microhabitat at station C6, dissolved oxygen was less than 5.0 mg/L on 20 days in 2008 for periods up to 7 hours and on 11 days in 2010 for periods up to 8.0 hours (fig. 12A and B, respectively).

Relatively low flows during the critical periods of 2008 and 2010 were associated with warmer, more stressful water temperatures to YOY smallmouth bass than were observed in 2009. Overall, river conditions in 2009 were relatively cool and apparently not conducive to disease occurrence. Diseased YOY smallmouth bass that were discovered by PFBC biologists in 2009 were living primarily within the areas of warm-water discharges (Geoffrey Smith, Pennsylvania Fish and Boat Commission, oral commun., 2009). Median daily maximum water temperatures in 2008 and 2010 in the main-channel habitat of the Susquehanna River at station C8 were 4.0 and 4.3°C warmer than in 2009 (fig. 9D, E, and F). Water temperatures in the main-channel habitat of the Juniata River at station C5 were 3.5°C warmer in 2008 than in 2009 and 3.3°C warmer in 2010 than 2009 (fig. 10D, E, and F).

Although most research relating to pH stress has focused on acidic conditions rather than near-neutral or alkaline conditions, Scott and others (2005) determined that perch (*Perca fluviatilis*), a warm-water fish that coexists with smallmouth bass in inland lakes, can experience interruption of ammonia excretion in lakes with persistently high pH (up to 9.9). The pH in the study area rarely exceeded 9.0, and pH greater than 9.0 lasted for only short periods of time (hours). Therefore, the pH of streamwater in the study area is not expected to be stressful to YOY smallmouth bass.

The pH in main-channel habitat of the Susquehanna River at station C8 was similar throughout the study period, ranging from 7.3 to 9.2 in 2008, 7.2 to 9.1 in 2009, and 7.2 to 9.1 in 2010 (tables 1–1, 1–2, and 1–3). Median daily maximum pH for the critical period of each year ranged from 8.1 in 2008 to 8.5 in 2009 (fig. 9G, H, and I). The pH of main-channel habitat in the Juniata River at station C5 ranged from 7.3 to 9.2 in 2008, 6.8 to 9.0 in 2009, and 7.2 to 9.1 in 2010 (tables 1–1, 1–2, and 1–3). At this station, median daily maximum pH for the critical period of each year ranged from 8.3 in 2009 to 8.5 in 2008 and 2010 (fig. 10G, H, and I).

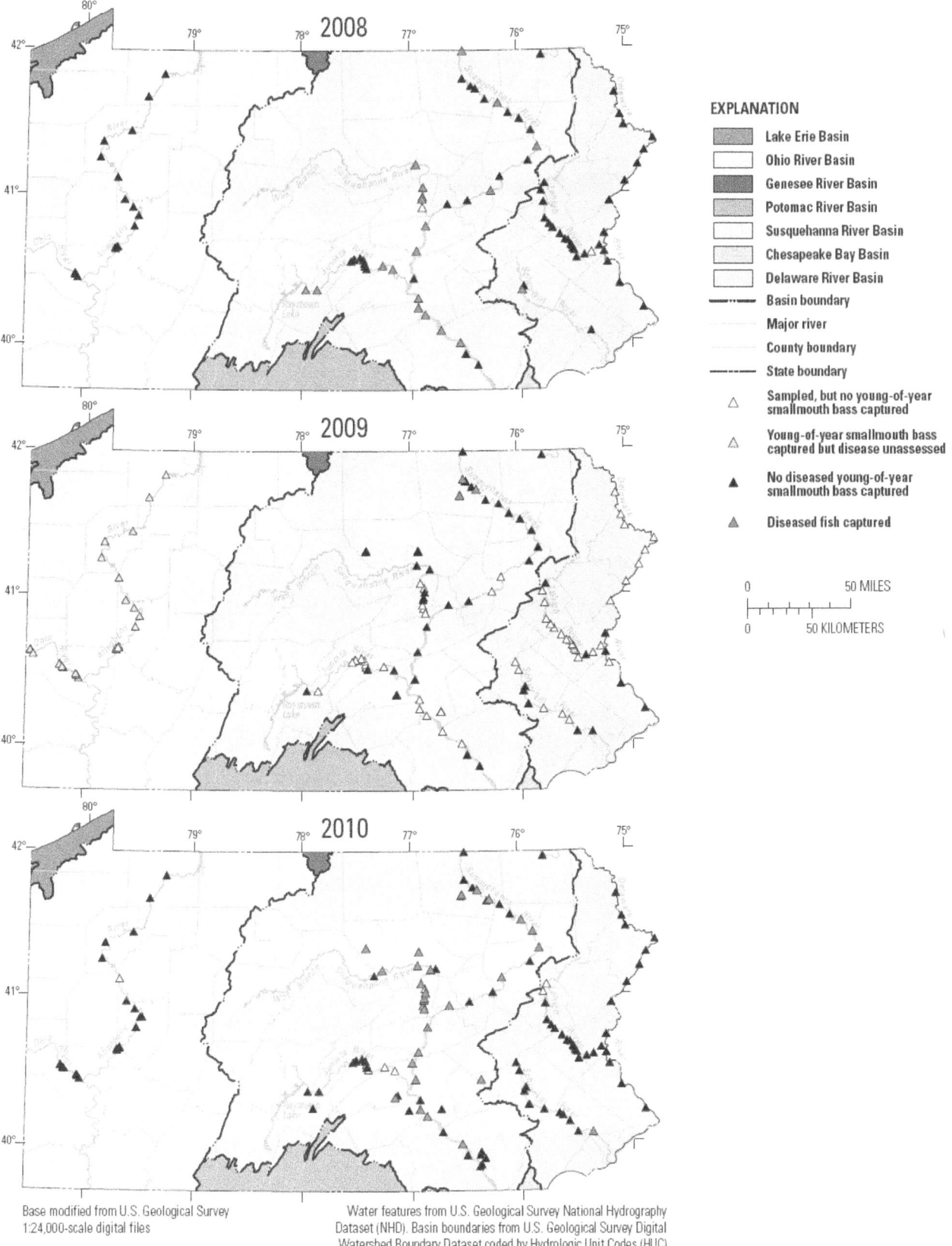

EXPLANATION

Lake Erie Basin
Ohio River Basin
Genesee River Basin
Potomac River Basin
Susquehanna River Basin
Chesapeake Bay Basin
Delaware River Basin
— Basin boundary
— Major river
— County boundary
— State boundary

△   Sampled, but no young-of-year
    smallmouth bass captured

△   Young-of-year smallmouth bass
    captured but disease unassessed

▲   No diseased young-of-year
    smallmouth bass captured

▲   Diseased fish captured

0   50 MILES

0   50 KILOMETERS

Base modified from U.S. Geological Survey
1:24,000-scale digital files

Water features from U.S. Geological Survey National Hydrography
Dataset (NHD). Basin boundaries from U.S. Geological Survey Digital
Watershed Boundary Dataset coded by Hydrologic Unit Codes (HUC)

Figure 8.   Geographic distribution of disease incidence in young-of-year smallmouth bass, Pennsylvania, 2008–10. (Data presented on the map for 2008 differ slightly from those presented on similar maps in Chaplin and others (2009) because of new information provided through written and oral communications from Geoffrey Smith, Pennsylvania Fish and Boat Commission, 2010)

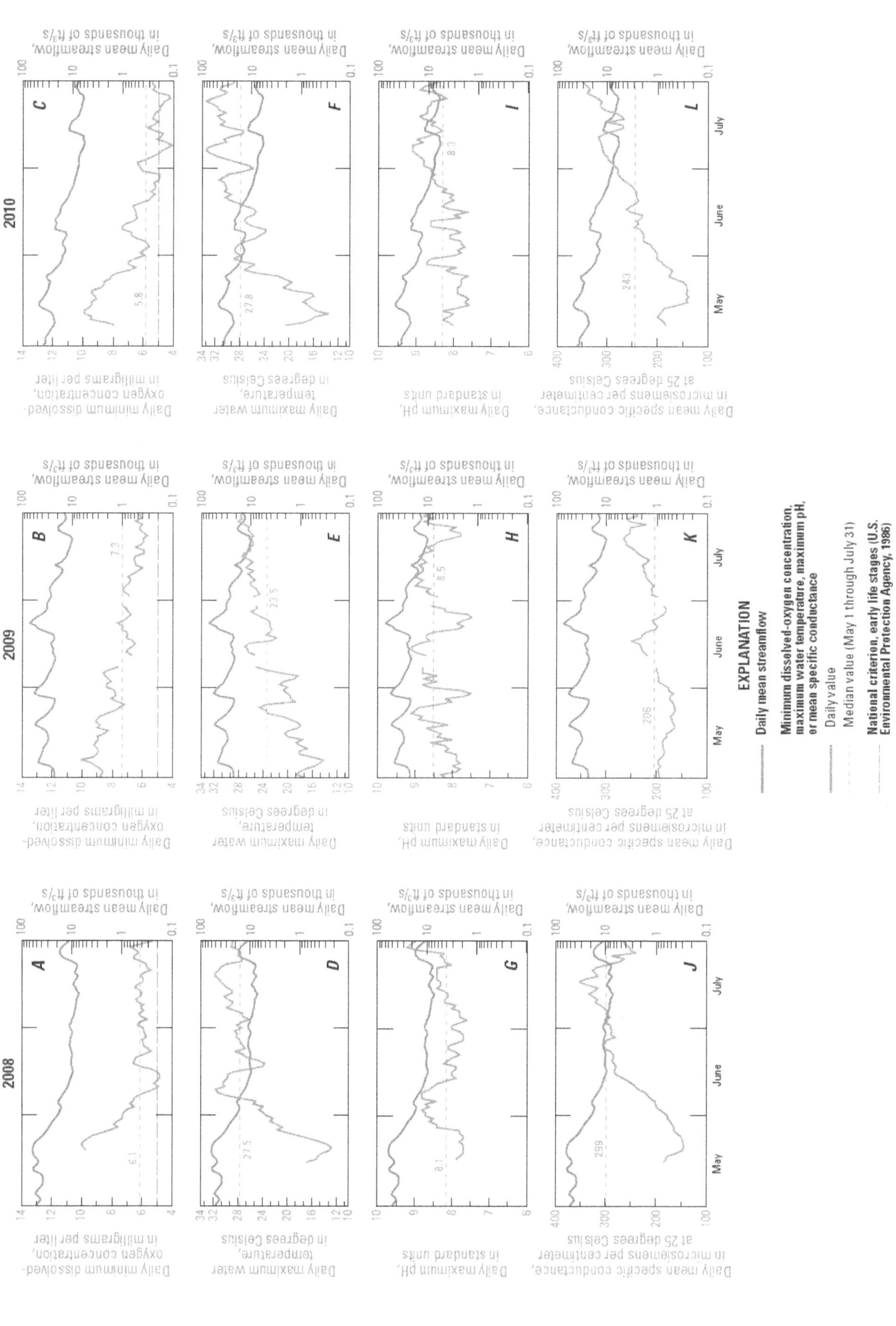

Figure 9.   Dissolved oxygen (*A–C*), water temperature (*D–F*), pH (*G–I*), and specific conductance (*J–L*) in the Susquehanna River at Harrisburg, Pa. (station C8), 2008–10. [ft³/s, cubic feet per second]

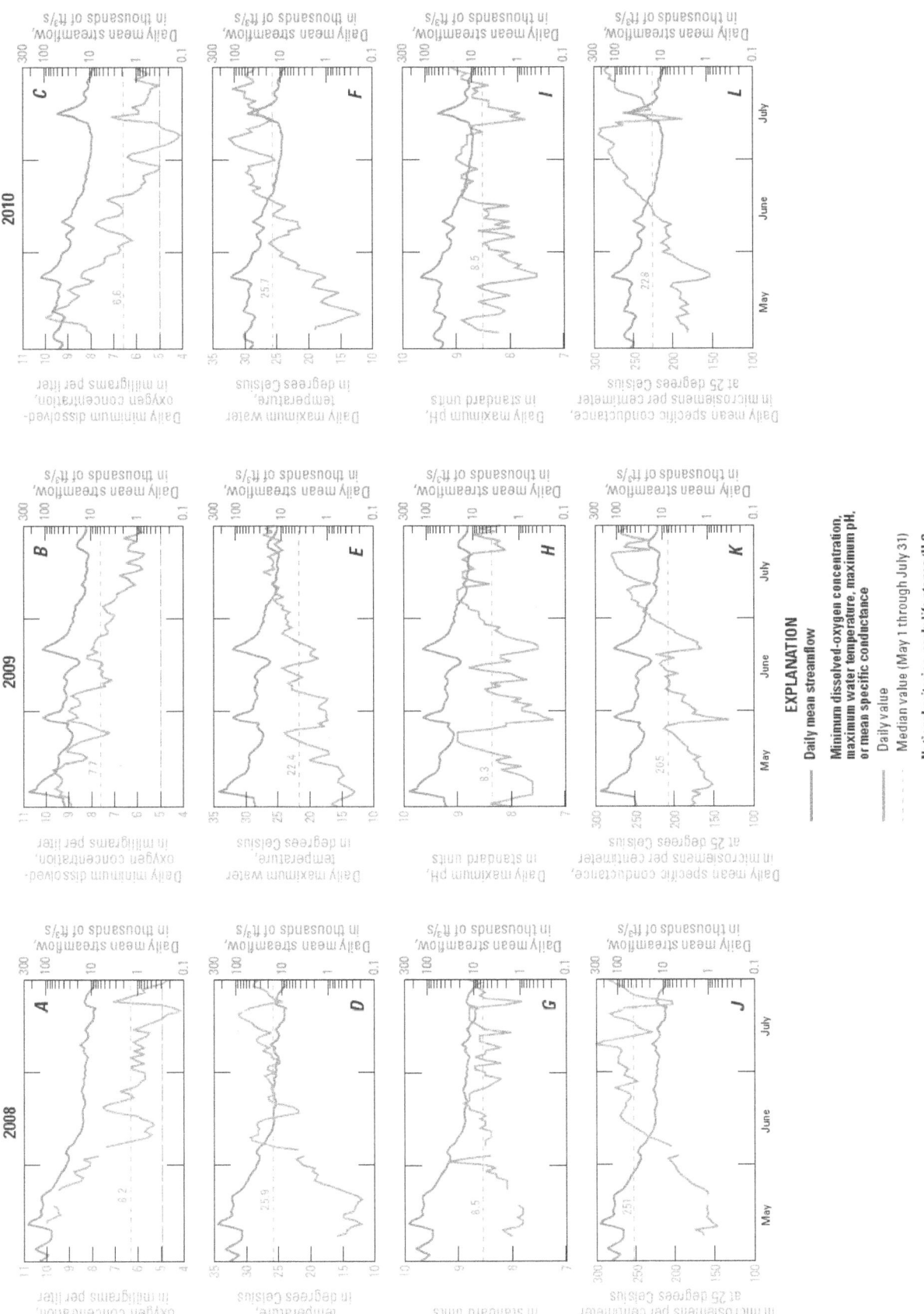

Figure 10. Dissolved oxygen (*A–C*), water temperature (*D–F*), pH (*G–I*), and specific conductance (*J–L*) in the Juniata River at Newport, Pa. (station C5), 2008–10. [ft³/s, cubic feet per second]

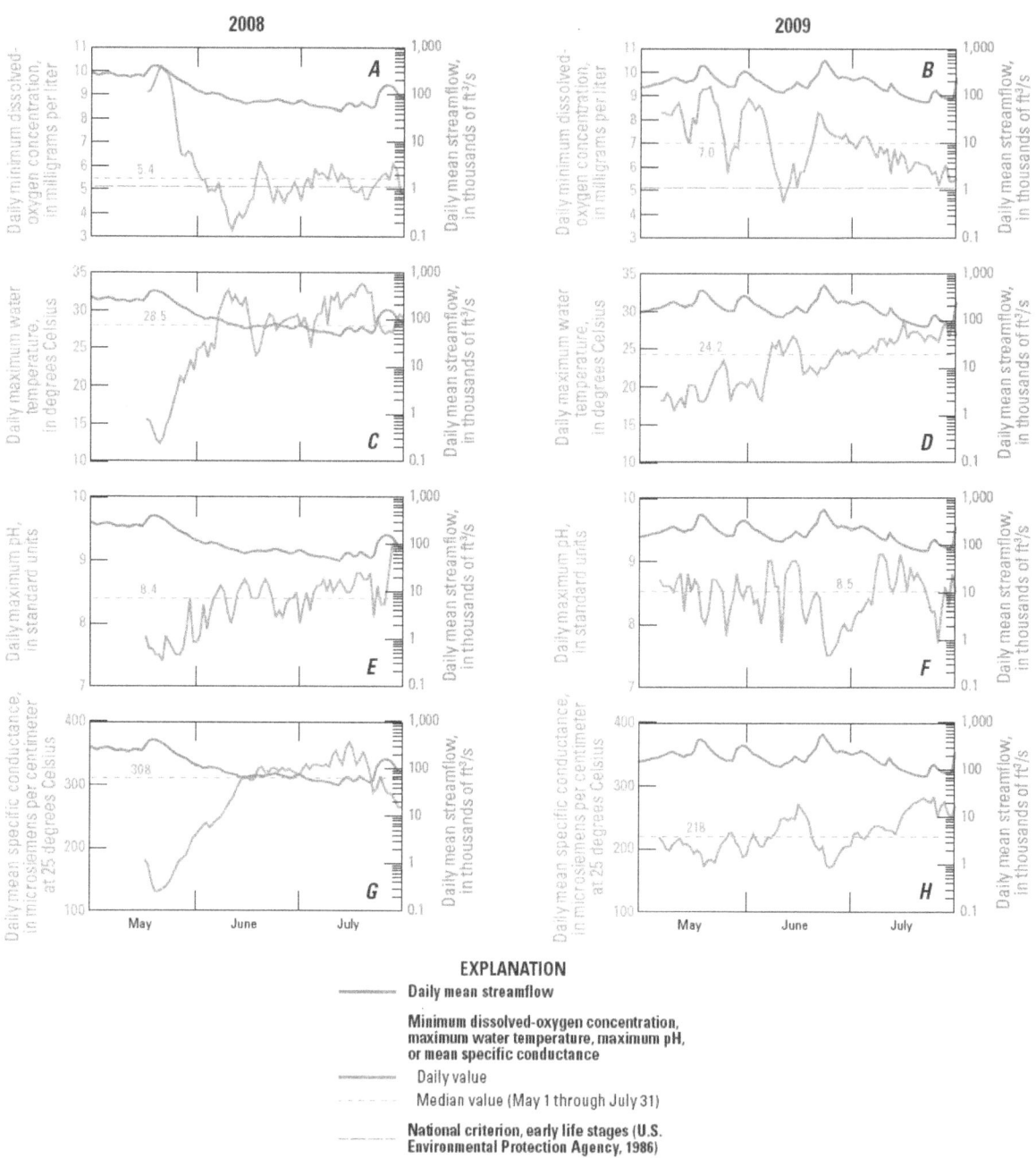

Figure 11. Dissolved oxygen (*A* and *B*), water temperature (*C* and *D*), pH (*E* and *F*), and specific conductance (*G* and *H*) in the Susquehanna River at Clemson Island, Pa. (station C4), 2008–09. [ft³/s, cubic feet per second; streamflow at station C4 is represented by flows measured at a streamgage on the Susquehanna River at Sunbury, Pa. (station N8), approximately 30 miles upstream]

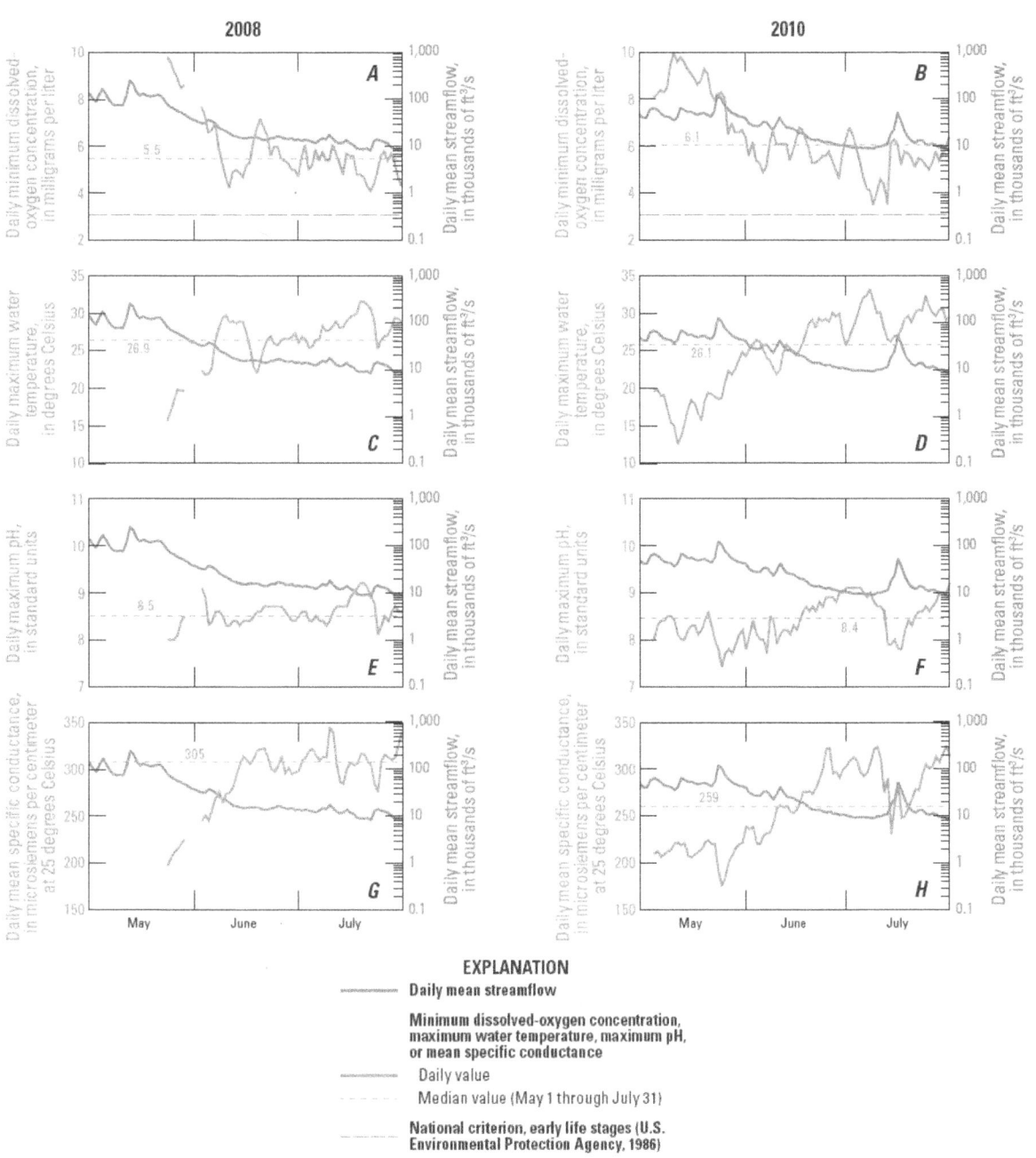

Figure 12. Dissolved oxygen (*A* and *B*), water temperature (*C* and *D*), pH (*E* and *F*), and specific conductance (*G* and *H*) in the Juniata River near Howe Township Park, Pa. (station C6), 2008 and 2010. [ft³/s, cubic feet per second; streamflow at station C6 is represented by flows measured at a streamgage on the Juniata River at Newport, Pa. (station C5), approximately 1 mile upstream]

The pH of microhabitat in the Susquehanna River at station C4 ranged from 7.1 to 9.3 in 2008 and 7.2 to 9.1 in 2009 (tables 1–1 and 1–2). The median daily maximum pHs for the critical periods of 2008 and 2009 were 8.4 and 8.5, respectively (fig. 11*E* and *F*). In the Juniata River microhabitat at station C6, pH was very similar to the values observed in the Susquehanna River, ranging from 7.3 to 9.2 in 2008 and 6.9 to 9.2 in 2010 (tables 1–1 and 1–3). The median daily maximums for the critical periods of 2008 and 2009 were 8.5 and 8.4, respectively (fig. 12*E* and *F*).

Specific conductance is a gross measure of the capacity of dissolved ions in water to conduct an electrical current (Wilde and others, 1998). Although linking specific conductance directly to fish health is difficult, it is related to the dissolved-solids concentration (Hem, 1985, p. 67) and can be used as a qualitative measure to distinguish between waters with high and low concentrations of dissolved solids. Ions dissolved in the water that may contribute to specific conductance include dissolved nutrients, sulfate, chloride and other salts, and metals. Nutrient and metal concentrations are known to fluctuate in concentration during the day (Scholefield and others, 2005; Nimick and others, 2005) in response to changes like those observed in this study for water temperature, pH, and dissolved oxygen.

Daily mean specific conductance varied as a function of streamflow and location. In the Susquehanna River at Harrisburg (station C8; fig. 9*J*, *K*, and *L*) and Juniata River at Newport (station C5; fig. 10*J*, *K*, and *L*), specific conductance was highest in the critical period of 2008 (medians of 299 µS/cm and 251 µS/cm, respectively), when streamflow was relatively low and dissolved solids were concentrated. Specific conductance was lowest at stations C8 and C5 during the critical period of 2009 (medians of 206 µS/cm and 205 µS/cm, respectively) when streamflow was high because because dissolved-solids concentrations in runoff were relatively low.

Comparison of Streamflow and Water Quality in 2008, 2009, and 2010 with Available Historical Data

Continuous streamflow and water quality data collected by the USGS in the 1970s were compared to data collected by USGS in 2008 at station C8 using a two-sided Wilcoxon signed-rank test 8. The comparisons indicate some statistically significant differences (p-values <0.05) between the historical dataset (1974–79) and the study period (2008–10) for streamflow, dissolved oxygen, and water temperature. However, streamflows and associated water-quality characteristics at station C8 were highly variable from year to year (figs. 6 and 13), and the datasets used for the comparisons are small. Methods for continuous water-quality data collection have improved greatly since the 1970s, allowing for fewer missing daily values and greater confidence in the data collected during 2008–10. Continued streamflow and water-quality

data collection beyond 2010 is necessary to allow for a more thorough analysis of trends.

Daily streamflows during the critical period of 2008 did not differ from those of the historical dataset (p-value = 0.0952); however, streamflows in the critical period of 2009 were significantly higher than those for the historical dataset (p-value = 0.0002), and streamflows in 2010 were significantly lower (p-value <0.0001). Variability of streamflow during the critical period of 2008 (quantified by a standard deviation of 17,000 ft³/s) was higher than in 2009 (standard deviation of 12,700 ft³/s) and 2010 (standard deviation of 10,800 ft³/s). This could explain why the Wilcoxon signed-rank test did not indicate any significant difference between streamflows during the critical period of 2008 and the historical dataset.

Comparison of the historical dataset with the combined 2008–10 dataset (fig. 14) indicates that daily mean streamflows at station C8 were significantly lower in the study period (p-value <0.0001; table 2). Although lower streamflows for the combined 2008–10 dataset may help explain statistical differences in dissolved oxygen and water temperature between the two time periods, other factors such as long-term streamwater warming trends (Kaushal and others, 2010) also may play a role.

Daily minimum dissolved-oxygen concentrations at station C8 for all 3 years of the study were significantly lower than those for the historical dataset (p-values of 0.0001or less), even though streamflow was at times no different than (2008), higher than (2009), or lower than (2010) streamflow for the historical dataset (table 2). The differences in dissolved-oxygen concentrations were greatest in 2008 and 2010, the 2 years with critical periods characterized by relatively low streamflow and high water temperature. Comparisons using the 19 days that are common to the 2008, 2009, 2010, and historical datasets at station C8 indicate median daily minimum dissolved-oxygen concentrations were 1.4 mg/L lower in 2008 than in the historical dataset, 0.5 mg/L lower in 2009 than in the historical dataset, and 2.2 mg/L lower in 2010 than in the historical dataset. For the combined study-period dataset at station C8, daily minimum dissolved oxygen was 1.4 mg/L lower than in the historical dataset. These lower dissolved-oxygen concentrations were associated with warmer water temperatures.

Daily maximum water temperatures at station C8 were significantly warmer (p-values <0.05) during the critical periods of 2008, 2009, and 2010 than during the historical period (table 2). Results of a comparison of combined data for the critical periods of 2008–10 with the historical dataset also indicate daily maximum water temperatures were significantly warmer in the study period. The median daily maximum water temperature was 2.3°C warmer for the combined 2008–10 dataset than for the same days during 1974–79. These results are consistent with warming trends documented in seven streams in the northeastern United States, including the Potomac River, which drains to the Chesapeake Bay and has a robust water temperature dataset extending back to 1922 (Kaushal and others, 2010).

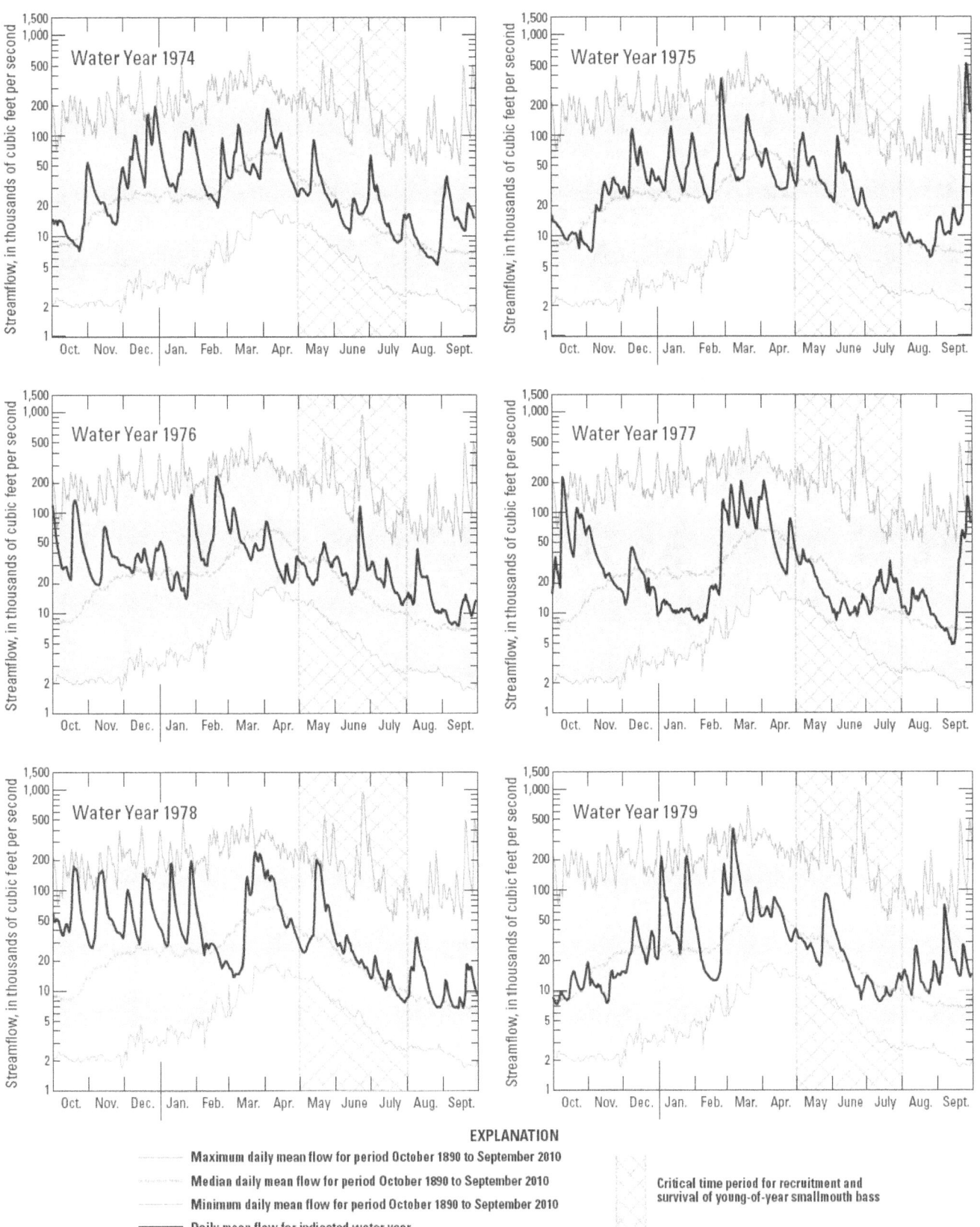

EXPLANATION

.... Maximum daily mean flow for period October 1890 to September 2010

.... Median daily mean flow for period October 1890 to September 2010

.... Minimum daily mean flow for period October 1890 to September 2010

—— Daily mean flow for indicated water year

Critical time period for recruitment and survival of young-of-year smallmouth bass

Figure 13. Streamflow in the Susquehanna River at Harrisburg, Pa. (station C8), during water years 1974, 1975, 1976, 1977, 1978, and 1979 compared to the range of streamflows for the entire period of record (1890–2010). (A water year extends from October 1– September 30 and is designated by the calendar year in which it ends.)

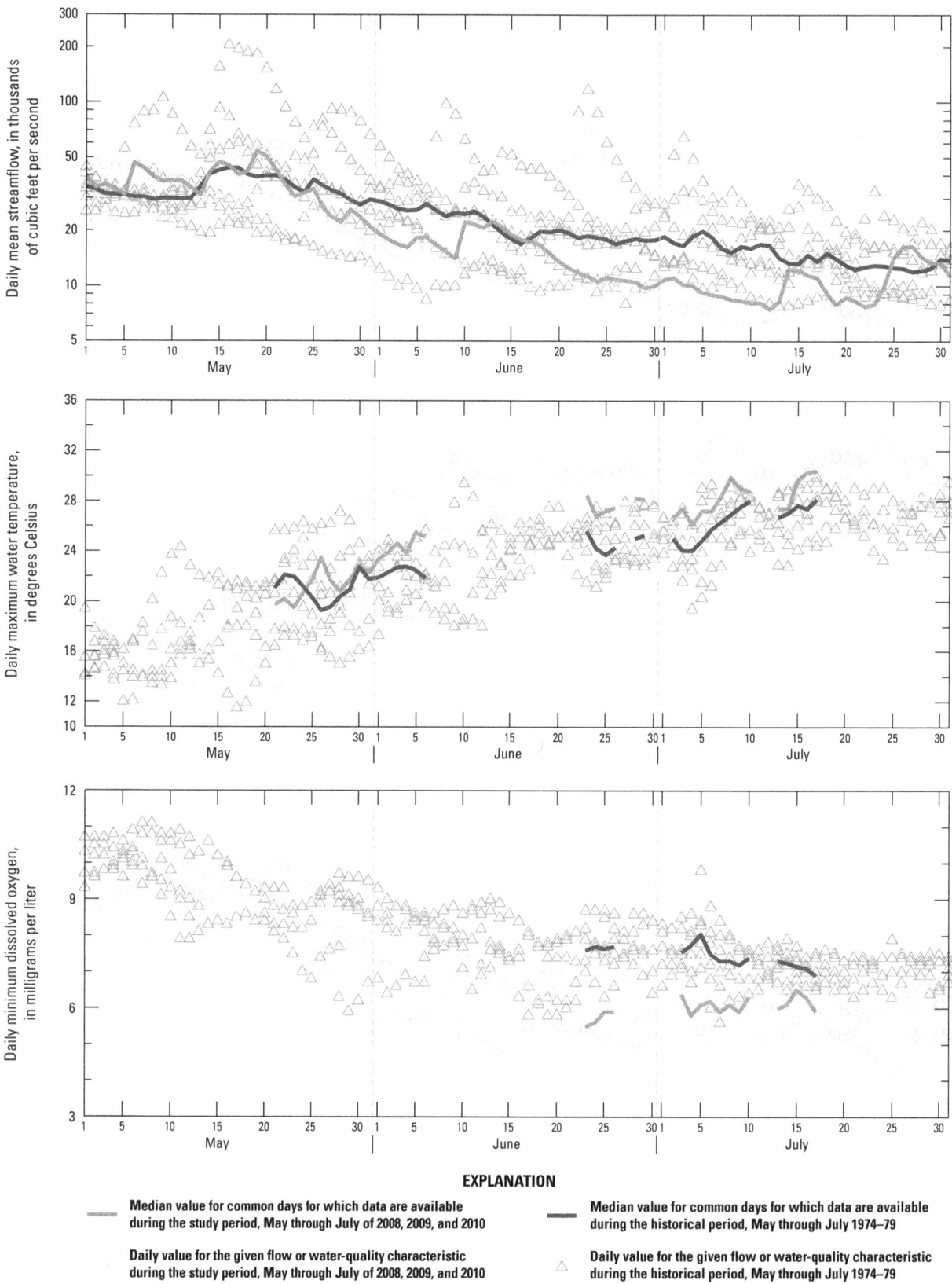

EXPLANATION

Median value for common days for which data are available during the study period, May through July of 2008, 2009, and 2010

Daily value for the given flow or water-quality characteristic during the study period, May through July of 2008, 2009, and 2010

Median value for common days for which data are available during the historical period, May through July 1974–79

Daily value for the given flow or water-quality characteristic during the historical period, May through July 1974–79

Figure 14.   Daily mean streamflow, daily maximum water temperature, and daily minimum dissolved oxygen for May through July of water years 1974–79 and 2008–10 in the Susquehanna River at Harrisburg, Pa. (station C8). (A water year extends from October 1–September 30 and is designated by the calendar year in which it ends.)

Table 2. Statistical results from comparison of 2008, 2009, and 2010 water-quality data to historical (1974–79) data for the Susquehanna River at Harrisburg, Pa. (station C8).

[N, number of samples; C, degrees Celsius; mg/L, milligrams per liter; ft³/s, cubic feet per second; <, less than; >, greater than; ns, no significant difference (p-value is greater than 0.05)]

Parameter	Susquehanna River at Harrisburg, 2008, compared to Susquehanna River at Harrisburg, historical[1]			Susquehanna River at Harrisburg, 2009, compared to Susquehanna River at Harrisburg, historical[1]			Susquehanna River at Harrisburg, 2010, compared to Susquehanna River at Harrisburg, historical[1]			Susquehanna River at Harrisburg, median 2008–10 compared to Susquehanna River at Harrisburg, historical[1]		
	p-value[2]	Direction of significance[3]	N	p-value[2]	Direction of significance[3]	N	p-value[2]	Direction of significance[3]	N	p-value[2]	Direction of significance[3]	N
Mean streamflow (ft³/s)	0.0952	ns	92	0.0002	>	92	<0.0001	<	92	<0.0001	<	92
Minimum dissolved oxygen (mg/L)	0.0001	<	19	<0.0001	<	19	0.0001	<	19	<0.0001	<	19
Maximum dissolved oxygen (mg/L)	<0.0001	<	20	0.3759	ns	19	0.4688	ns	19	0.8906	ns	19
Dissolved-oxygen range (mg/L)	0.0006	>	20	0.0031	>	19	0.0001	>	19	<0.0001	>	19
Mean dissolved oxygen (mg/L)	<0.0001	<	20	0.2935	ns	19	<0.0001	<	19	<0.0001	<	19
Minimum water temperature (°C)	0.0132	>	39	0.0066	<	37	<0.0001	>	37	0.0660	ns	37
Maximum water temperature (°C)	0.0021	>	39	0.0232	>	37	<0.0001	>	37	<0.0001	>	37
Water temperature range (°C)	0.0083	>	39	0.9940	ns	37	0.0001	>	37	0.0024	>	37
Mean water temperature (°C)	0.0056	>	39	0.0158	<	37	<0.0001	>	37	<0.0001	>	37

[1] Results of two-sided Wilcoxon signed-rank tests. For historical data, the medians of daily values computed from May 1 to July 31, 1974–79, are used. Only days that had data in all 7 years were included in this analysis. As a result, some characteristics could not be tested because there were too few data (N<19).

[2] For this study, a statistically significant difference exists if the p-value is less than 0.05.

[3] Indicates whether the value of the parameter in the given year(s) is significantly greater than or less than the historical data value.

Differences in Dissolved Oxygen and Water Temperature among the Susquehanna, Delaware, and Allegheny Rivers, 2008–10

At this time (2010), bacterial infections and associated lesions are believed to be most prevalent in the Susquehanna River Basin. In this section, differences in water quality characteristics among the basins are explored as a possible explanation for the higher incidence of disease in the Susquehanna River basin. Water-temperature, dissolved-oxygen, and pH data collected in the Susquehanna River at station C8 are compared with corresponding data from the Delaware River at Trenton, N.J. (station C1), and the Allegheny River at Acmetonia, Pa. (station C10).

Regardless of year-to-year variability in streamflow, daily minimum dissolved oxygen at station C8 was consistently lower than at stations C1 and C10, especially in June and July of each year (fig. 15). Median daily minimum dissolved-oxygen concentrations during the critical period at station C8 were 6.1 mg/L in 2008, 7.3 mg/L in 2009, and 5.8 mg/L in 2010 (tables 1–1, 1–2, and 1–3) compared to 7.8, 8.7, and 7.8 mg/L, respectively, at station C1 (tables 2–1, 2–2, and 2–3). Station C10 had median daily minimum dissolved-oxygen concentrations that were greater than those at station C8 but lower than those at station C1; median daily minimum values at station C10 were 7.1 mg/L in 2008, 7.6 mg/L in 2009, and 7.1 mg/L in 2010. Dissolved oxygen did not fall below the U.S. Environmental Protection Agency (1986) criterion of 5.0 mg/L at station C1 or C10 during the study period. In contrast, dissolved oxygen at station C8 was at or below 5.0 mg/L on 5 days in 2008, no days in 2009, and 14 days in 2010.

Results of a comparison of water temperatures during the critical period of each year indicate that streamwater of the Susquehanna River at station C8 was usually warmer than that of the Allegheny River at station C10 and the Delaware River at station C1. Median daily maximum temperatures at station C8 were 2.0°C warmer than at station C1 in 2008, 2.7°C warmer in 2009, and 1.6°C warmer in 2010. Likewise, streamwater at station C8 was warmer than that at station C10 by 3.1°C in 2008, 1.2°C in 2009, and 3.4°C in 2010.

Summary and Conclusions

Since 2005, spring hatched young-of-year (YOY) smallmouth bass living in Pennsylvania reaches of the Susquehanna River have experienced widespread disease and above-normal mortality when summertime streamflows are near normal or lower. At this time (2010), widespread disease and mortality are believed to be more prevalent in the Susquehanna River Basin than in the Delaware or Allegheny River Basin. The symptoms of disease include skin lesions, gill necrosis, and fin rot, all occurring in varying degrees of severity. Reconnaissance water-quality monitoring by the Pennsylvania Fish and Boat Commission (PFBC) in the spring and summer of 2007 measured low dissolved-oxygen concentrations (<5.0 mg/L) in the Susquehanna River near Sunbury, Pa. In response to the mortalities and initial findings by PFBC, the U.S. Geological Survey (USGS) began a study in 2008 to investigate dissolved oxygen and water temperature as possible stressors to YOY smallmouth bass in affected reaches of the Susquehanna River. In cooperation with PFBC and the Pennsylvania Department of Environmental Protection, monitoring initiated in 2008 was continued in 2009 and 2010 in selected reaches of the river. Streamflow data from USGS streamgages and data collected from continuous (30-minute intervals) water-quality sondes measuring dissolved oxygen, water temperature, pH, and specific conductance were analyzed. The focus was on data for May 1 through July 31 of 2008, 2009, and 2010, the critical period for YOY smallmouth bass survival and development.

Near-normal or lower streamflows, like those during the critical periods of 2008 and 2010, were associated with lower dissolved-oxygen concentrations, warmer water temperatures, and increased incidence of disease compared to higher flows like those during the critical period of 2009. Median daily streamflows during the critical periods of 2008 and 2010 were approximately one-half the streamflow for the same period in 2009—13,100 ft³/s and 14,300 ft³/s in 2008 and 2010, respectively, compared to 26,300 ft³/s in 2009. These streamflows were associated with the capture of diseased YOY smallmouth bass at 19 and 28 sites in 2008 and 2010, respectively, but only 3 sites in 2009.

Datasets for this study are relatively small and trends that have been documented in other tributaries to the Chesapeake Bay, such as streamwater warming, are not well established for the Susquehanna River. Nonetheless, the effect of warming streamwater in the Susquehanna River could be superimposed on the influence of yearly streamflow fluctuation. If warming is occurring in the Susquehanna River, the same magnitude of streamflow today may result in water-quality characteristics that are more stressful than they would have been decades ago.

During conditions of relatively low streamflow in the critical periods of 2008 and 2010, dissolved-oxygen concentrations were lower (more stressful to aquatic life) than in 2009. During the critical periods of 2008 and 2010, median daily minimum dissolved-oxygen concentrations in main-channel habitat of the Susquehanna River at Harrisburg (station C8) were 1.2 mg/L and 1.5 mg/L lower, respectively, than in 2009. Despite the year-to-year differences, comparison of water-quality data for each year of the study period with historical data available for station C8 from 1974–79 indicates daily minimum dissolved-oxygen concentrations were significantly lower in all 3 years of the study (p-values <0.05). This was the case even though streamflow was at times no different than (2008), significantly higher than (2009), or significantly lower than (2010) streamflow in the historical dataset.

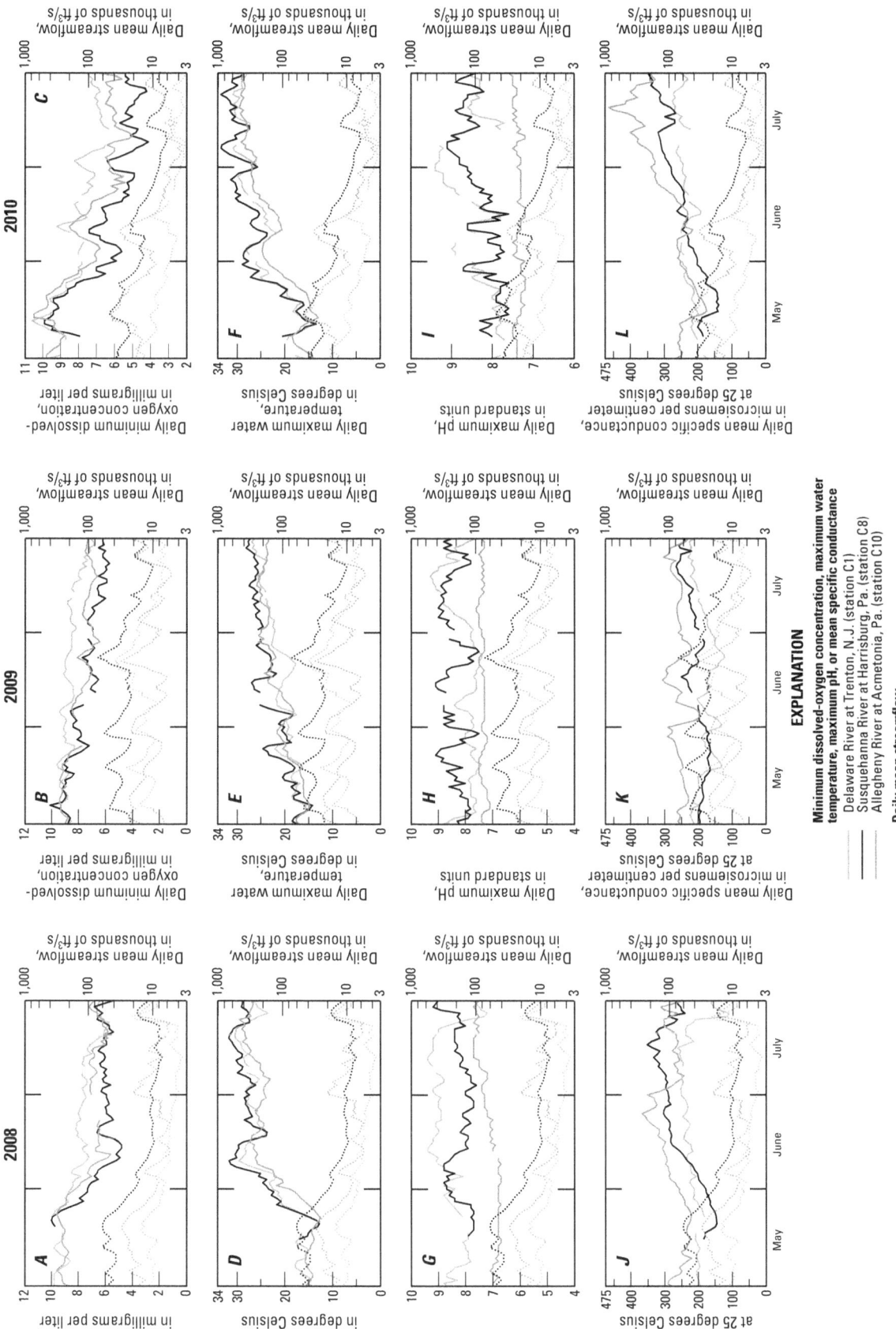

Figure 15. Water-quality characteristics and streamflow for the Susquehanna River at Harrisburg, Pa. (station C8); Delaware River at Trenton, N.J. (station C1); and Allegheny River at Acmetonia, Pa. (station C10), 2008–10. [ft³/s, cubic feet per second; streamflow at station C10 is represented by flows measured at a streamgage on the Allegheny River at Natrona, Pa. (station C9), approximately 10 miles upstream]

Along with lower dissolved-oxygen concentrations, warmer, more stressful water temperatures also were observed in 2008 and 2010 compared to 2009. Median daily maximum water temperatures in the main channel of the Susquehanna River at station C8 were 4.0°C warmer in 2008 and 4.3°C warmer in 2010 than in 2009 during the critical periods. In main-channel habitat of the Juniata River at station C5, critical-period water temperatures were 3.5°C warmer in 2008 and 3.3°C warmer in 2010 than in 2009. Comparison of water temperatures at station C8 with those in the historical dataset from 1974–79 indicates all three study-period years had significantly warmer critical-period water temperatures (p-values <0.05).

During the critical period of each year, YOY smallmouth bass microhabitats, characterized by shallow, slow-moving water in nearshore areas, had lower dissolved-oxygen concentrations than nearby main-channel habitats. Few year-to-year comparisons can be made for microhabitats because water-quality data were not collected over all 3 years of the study period. Data that are available indicate that the median daily minimum dissolved-oxygen concentration at the microhabitat in the Susquehanna River at Clemson Island (station C4) was 1.6 mg/L lower during the critical period of 2008 than in the same timeframe in 2009. No data were collected at station C4 in 2010. Water-quality data are available for the microhabitat in the Juniata River at Howe Township Park (station C6) in 2008 and 2010 only. Median daily minimum dissolved-oxygen concentrations were about 0.6 mg/L lower in 2008 than in 2010.

In 2008 at station C4 and in 2010 at station C6, concentrations of dissolved oxygen sometimes were lower than the 5.0-mg/L criterion established by the U.S. Environmental Protection Agency for early life stages of warm-water fish. Daily minimum dissolved-oxygen concentrations during the study period were lower than 5.0 mg/L for as many as 31 of 92 days during the critical period (station C4 in 2008). The longest duration for which dissolved oxygen was lower than 5.0 mg/L was 8.5 hours (station C4; 23:30 on June 10, 2008, to 08:00 on June 11, 2008).

For the critical period of each year, dissolved oxygen was consistently lower and water temperatures were consistently warmer in the Susquehanna River at station C8 than in the Delaware River at station C1 and the Allegheny River at station C10, especially in June and July of each year. The median daily minimum dissolved-oxygen concentration during the critical period at station C8 was 6.1 mg/L in 2008, 7.3 mg/L in 2009, and 5.8 mg/L in 2010, whereas concentrations were 7.8, 8.7, and 7.8 mg/L, respectively, in the Delaware River at station C1. Daily minimum dissolved-oxygen concentrations in the Allegheny River at station C10 were greater than concentrations in the Susquehanna River at station C8, but lower than those in the Delaware River at station C1; median daily minimum values at station C10 were 7.1°C in 2008, 7.6°C in 2009, and 7.1°C in 2010. Water temperatures at station C8 within the critical period of each year typically were warmer than in the Delaware River at station C1;

median daily maximum temperatures at station C8 were 2.0°C warmer than at station C1 in 2008, 2.7°C warmer in 2009, and 1.6°C warmer in 2010. Comparison of median daily maximum water temperatures within the critical period of each year indicates the Susquehanna River at station C8 typically was warmer than the Allegheny River at station C10 by 3.1°C in 2008, 1.2°C in 2009, and 3.4°C in 2010.

In conclusion, the data collected during this study indicate the following: (1) Microhabitats where YOY smallmouth bass live have lower dissolved oxygen, contributing to more stressful conditions to aquatic life, than are observed in the main-channel habitats, even during critical periods with relatively high streamflow (such as 2009). (2) Dissolved-oxygen concentrations and water temperatures are associated with streamflow, with lower dissolved oxygen and higher water temperatures in years with relatively low flow such as 2008 and 2010. (3) Dissolved oxygen was significantly lower and water temperature was significantly higher during 2008–10 compared to historical conditions during 1974–79. (4) Under higher flow conditions like those experienced in 2009, increased dissolved oxygen and cooler water temperatures were observed in all three major rivers; however, the Susquehanna River still had lower dissolved-oxygen concentrations and warmer water temperatures than the Delaware or Allegheny River. (5) Specific conductance and pH in the Susquehanna River are within the range of fluctuations observed in the Delaware and Allegheny Rivers and are not expected to be major stressors linked to the occurrence of disease in YOY smallmouth bass.

Acknowledgments

The cooperation, guidance, and support from Pennsylvania Fish and Boat Commission (PFBC) and Pennsylvania Department of Environmental Protection (PADEP) for study efforts in 2008 are gratefully acknowledged. For continuation of the study in 2009 and 2010, John Arway and Geoff Smith served as the study directors for the PFBC and contributed scientific expertise, ideas, and coordination skills to help make the project successful. Michael Burton of the Pennsylvania Bass Federation and Geoff Smith contributed time, equipment, and expertise as boat operators for the project. Robert Lorantas of the PFBC is acknowledged for contributions of annual survey data for YOY smallmouth bass across Pennsylvania.

Many individuals in the PADEP are recognized for their contributions, including Richard Shertzer, Robert Schott, Joseph Hepp, and Michael (Joshua) Lookenbill. Staff from the Susquehanna River Basin Commission, including David Heicher and Andrew Gavin, also are recognized for their contributions to this study. Linda Zarr, Joanne Irvin, David Smith, Randall Conger, and Joseph Cukjati of the U.S. Geological survey assisted with the data collection, compilation, management, and graphics-presentation tasks. USGS reviewers Robin Brightbill and Kimberly Shaffer, along with Rodney Kime of PADEP and Geoffrey Smith of PFBC, offered valuable suggestions for improving the report.

References Cited

Chaplin, J.J., Crawford, J.K., and Brightbill, R.A., 2009, Water quality monitoring in response to young-of-the-year smallmouth bass (*Micropterus dolomieu*) mortality in the Susquehanna River and major tributaries, Pennsylvania: 2008: U.S. Geological Survey Open-File Report 2009–1216, 59 p.

Decostere, A., Haesebrouck, F., Turnbull, J.F., and Charlier, G., 1999, Influence of water quality and temperature on adhesion of high and low virulence *Flavobacterium columnare* strains to isolated gill arches: Journal of Fish Diseases, v. 22, p. 1–11.

Durborow, R.M., Thune, R.L., Hawke, J.P., and Camus, A.C., 1998, Columnaris disease—A bacterial infection caused by *Flavobacterium columnare*: Southern Regional Aquaculture Center, no. 479, 4 p.

Garman, Greg, and Orth, Donald, 2007, Fish kills in the Shenandoah River basin—Preliminary report of the Shenandoah River basin Science Team: Virginia Department of Environmental Quality, Va., 16 p.

Helsel, D.R., and Hirsch, R.M., 2002, Statistical methods in water resources: U.S. Geological Survey Techniques of Water-Resources Investigations, book 4, chap. A3, p. 118–124 and 142–147.

Hem, J.D., 1985, Study and interpretation of the chemical characteristics of natural water (3d ed.): U.S. Geological Survey Water-Supply Paper 2254, 263 p.

Kaushal, S.S., Likens, G.E., Jaworski, N.A., Pace, M.L., Sides, A.M., Seekell, D., Belt, K.T., Secor, D.H., and Wingate, R.L., 2010, Rising stream and river temperatures in the United States: Frontiers in Ecology and the Environment, v. 8, p. 461-466.

Maule, A.G., and Schreck, C.B., 1990, Changes in number of leukocytes in immune organs of juvenile coho salmon (*Oncorhynchus kisutch*) after acute stress or cortisol treatment: Journal of Aquatic Animal Health, v. 2, p. 298–304.

Nimick, D.A., Cleasby, T.E., and McCleskey, R.B., 2005, Seasonality of diel cycles of dissolved metal concentrations in a Rocky Mountain stream: Environmental Geology, v. 47, p. 603–614.

Pennsylvania Fish and Boat Commission, 2005, As research continues into causes and effects of smallmouth bass dieoff, young of the year analysis provides encouraging news, accessed July 10, 2009, at *http://www.fish.state.pa.us/news-releases/2005/smb_yoy.htm*.

Pennsylvania Fish and Boat Commission, 2009, Pennsylvania fishes, accessed January 11, 2011, at *http://www.fish.state.pa.us/pafish/fishhtms/chapindx.htm*.

Ripley, J., Iwanowicz, L., Blazer, V., and Foran, C., 2008, Utilization of protein expression profiles as indicators of environmental impairment of smallmouth bass (*Micropterus dolomieui*) from the Shenandoah River, Virginia, USA: Environmental Toxicology and Chemistry, v. 27, no. 8, p. 1756–1767.

Scholefield, David, Goff, T.L., Braven, Jim, Ebdon, Les, Long, Terry, and Butler, Mark, 2005, Concerted diurnal patterns in riverine nutrient concentrations and physical conditions: Science of the Total Environment, v. 344, p. 201–210.

Scott, D.M., Lucas, M.C., and Wilson, R.W., 2005, The effect of high pH on ion balance, nitrogen excretion, and behavior in freshwater fish from an eutrophic lake—A laboratory and field study: Aquatic Toxicology, v. 73, p. 31–43.

U.S. Environmental Protection Agency, 1986, Ambient water quality criteria for dissolved oxygen: Washington, D.C., U.S. Environmental Protection Agency, Office of Water Regulations and Standards, Criteria and Standards Division, EPA 440/5-86-003, April 1986, 46 p., accessed May 3, 2011, at *http://nepis.epa.gov/Exe/ZyPURL.cgi?Dockey=00001MSS.txt*.

U.S. Geological Survey, 2003, User's manual for the National Water Information System of the U.S. Geological Survey automated data processing system (ADAPS): U.S. Geological Survey Open-File Report 03–123, version 4.3, 407 p.

Wagner, R.J., Boulger, R.W., Jr., Oblinger, C.J., and Smith, B.A., 2006, Guidelines and standard procedures for continuous water quality monitors—Station operation, record computation, and data reporting: U.S. Geological Survey Techniques and Methods I-D3, 51 p. plus attachments.

Wang, W.B., Li, A.H., Cai, T.Z., and Wang, J.G., 2005, Effects of intraperitoneal injection of cortisol on nonspecific immune functions of *Ctenopharyngodon idella*: Journal of Fish Biology, v. 67, p.779–793.

Wilde, R.D., Radtke, D.B., Gibs, J., and Iwatsubo, R.T., 1998, National field manual for the collection of water quality data: U.S. Geological Survey Techniques of Water-Resources Investigations, book 9, variously paged.

Yellow Springs Instruments, 1999, Environmental monitoring systems operations manual: Yellow Springs, Ohio, 264 p.

Appendixes 1–2

Appendix 1.   Summary Statistics for Water-Quality Data Collected in the Susquehanna River Basin

Table 1–1.   Summary statistics for water-quality data collected at selected sampling stations in the Susquehanna River Basin, Pennsylvania, May 1 through July 31, 2008.

[C3, Susquehanna River below Clemson Island (Main Channel); C4, Susquehanna River at Clemson Island (Microhabitat); C5, Juniata River at Newport; C6, Juniata River near Howe Township Park (Microhabitat); C7, Juniata River near Howe Township Park (Main Channel); C8, Susquehanna River at Harrisburg; C, degrees Celsius; µS/cm, microsiemens per centimeter; mg/L, milligrams per liter; n, number of daily values; P25, 25th percentile; P75, 75th percentile]

Statistic	Daily minimum temperature (°C)						Daily mean temperature (°C)						Daily maximum temperature (°C)						Daily temperature range (°C)					
	C3	C4	C5	C6	C7	C8	C3	C4	C5	C6	C7	C8	C3	C4	C5	C6	C7	C8	C3	C4	C5	C6	C7	C8
n	76	76	81	65	57	77	76	76	80	65	57	77	76	76	83	65	57	77	76	76	80	65	57	77
Minimum	10.9	11.0	10.9	13.5	19.5	11.8	11.8	11.8	11.5	14.5	21.0	12.2	12.4	12.4	12.0	15.6	22.4	12.8	1.0	1.1	0.8	0.9	1.6	0.6
P25	20.7	20.4	18.3	22.6	23.6	21.7	22.5	22.4	18.8	24.1	25.0	23.0	25.0	24.9	19.4	25.5	26.6	23.9	3.4	3.3	2.3	2.3	2.5	2.1
Median	24.1	23.7	22.6	24.0	24.8	25.2	26.1	25.8	24.3	25.5	26.4	26.3	28.4	28.5	25.9	26.9	27.8	27.5	4.3	4.8	3.1	3.0	3.2	2.7
P75	25.5	24.9	24.0	25.8	26.0	26.4	27.6	27.4	26.0	27.3	27.6	28.0	30.5	30.8	27.6	28.8	29.3	29.6	5.5	6.2	3.9	3.4	3.6	3.2
Maximum	27.7	27.0	26.4	27.5	27.8	29.2	29.9	29.7	28.7	29.5	29.6	30.3	32.8	33.5	31.2	31.5	31.8	31.7	6.8	7.9	5.9	6.3	5.2	4.1
Mean	22.5	22.1	20.6	23.4	24.6	23.4	24.4	24.2	22.1	24.9	26.1	24.6	26.7	26.8	23.4	26.4	27.7	26.0	4.2	4.7	3.1	3.0	3.1	2.6
Standard deviation	4.5	4.2	4.7	3.1	1.9	4.7	4.8	4.7	5.1	3.3	2.0	4.9	5.3	5.5	5.7	3.4	2.2	5	1.4	1.9	1.2	0.9	0.8	1

Statistic	Daily minimum dissolved oxygen (mg/L)						Daily mean dissolved oxygen (mg/L)						Daily maximum dissolved oxygen (mg/L)						Daily dissolved oxygen range (mg/L)					
	C3	C4	C5	C6	C7	C8	C3	C4	C5	C6	C7	C8	C3	C4	C5	C6	C7	C8	C3	C4	C5	C6	C7	C8
n	76	76	74	65	57	73	76	76	74	65	57	73	76	76	74	65	58	73	76	76	74	65	57	73
Minimum	5.3	3.3	4.1	4.1	4.6	4.8	7.5	5.8	6.6	6.0	6.6	6.1	9.5	8.2	8.2	8.2	9.1	7.3	0.6	0.6	0.3	0.6	2.0	0.3
P25	6.0	4.9	5.7	5.0	5.5	5.9	8.0	7.0	8.1	7.2	8.2	6.9	10.3	9.1	10.3	9.3	10.5	8.2	3.3	3.3	3.1	3.4	4.5	2.0
Median	6.4	5.4	6.2	5.5	6.0	6.1	8.4	7.3	8.5	7.8	8.6	7.4	10.6	9.5	11.1	10.1	11.5	8.6	4.1	4.4	4.9	4.3	5.4	2.3
P75	7.3	5.9	7.7	6.1	6.4	6.6	8.9	7.8	9.4	8.3	9.0	8.1	11.0	10.5	12.2	10.7	12.5	9.4	4.9	5.0	5.9	4.8	6.3	2.7
Maximum	10.3	10.2	10.0	9.8	7.9	10.0	11.1	10.5	10.3	10.1	10.3	10.2	15.2	12.5	13.3	11.8	13.6	10.7	7.7	6.4	8.6	7.3	8.9	3.9
Mean	6.8	5.7	6.7	5.8	6.1	6.5	8.6	7.6	8.7	7.9	8.6	7.6	10.7	9.7	11.2	9.9	11.5	8.8	3.9	4.0	4.5	4.1	5.4	2.3
Standard deviation	1.4	1.6	1.5	1.3	0.8	1.2	0.9	1.1	0.9	0.9	0.7	0.9	0.8	0.9	1.1	0.9	1.2	1	1.5	1.5	2.2	1.4	1.4	1

Table 1–1. Summary statistics for water-quality data collected at selected sampling stations in the Susquehanna River Basin, Pennsylvania, May 1 through July 31, 2008.—Continued

[C3, Susquehanna River below Clemson Island (Main Channel); C4, Susquehanna River at Clemson Island (Microhabitat); C5, Juniata River at Newport; C6, Juniata River near Howe Township Park (Microhabitat); C7, Juniata River near Howe Township Park (Main Channel); C8, Susquehanna River at Harrisburg; C, degrees Celsius; μS/cm, microsiemens per centimeter; mg/L, milligrams per liter; n, number of daily values; P25, 25th percentile; P75, 75th percentile]

Daily minimum pH (standard units)

Statistic	C3	C4	C5	C6	C7	C8
n	76	76	79	65	57	76
Minimum	7.4	7.1	7.3	7.3	7.6	7.3
P25	7.7	7.3	7.5	7.7	7.8	7.5
Median	7.8	7.4	7.6	7.8	7.9	7.5
P75	7.8	7.5	7.7	8.0	8.1	7.6
Maximum	8.9	8.5	8.3	8.6	8.3	8.7
Mean	7.8	7.4	7.6	7.9	7.9	7.6
Standard deviation	0.3	0.2	0.2	0.2	0.2	0.2

Daily median pH (standard units)

Statistic	C3	C4	C5	C6	C7	C8
n	76	76	79	65	57	76
Minimum	7.5	7.3	7.5	7.6	7.9	7.5
P25	8.2	7.6	7.8	8.0	8.2	7.6
Median	8.3	7.8	8.0	8.2	8.4	7.8
P75	8.5	7.9	8.1	8.4	8.6	8.0
Maximum	9.2	9.0	8.5	9.0	8.7	8.9
Mean	8.3	7.8	8.0	8.2	8.4	7.9
Standard deviation	0.4	0.3	0.2	0.3	0.2	0.3

Daily maximum pH (standard units)

Statistic	C3	C4	C5	C6	C7	C8
n	76	76	79	65	57	76
Minimum	7.6	7.4	7.8	8.0	8.4	7.6
P25	8.6	8.1	8.2	8.4	8.6	7.8
Median	8.8	8.4	8.5	8.5	8.7	8.1
P75	8.9	8.6	8.7	8.7	8.8	8.4
Maximum	9.4	9.3	9.2	9.2	9.0	9.2
Mean	8.7	8.3	8.4	8.6	8.7	8.2
Standard deviation	0.4	0.4	0.3	0.3	0.2	0.4

Daily pH range (standard units)

Statistic	C3	C4	C5	C6	C7	C8
n	76	76	79	65	57	76
Minimum	0.2	0.1	0.1	0.2	0.2	0.1
P25	0.8	0.7	0.6	0.6	0.7	0.4
Median	0.9	0.9	0.9	0.7	0.8	0.6
P75	1.1	1.1	1.0	0.8	0.9	0.8
Maximum	1.5	1.6	1.3	1.4	1.1	1.3
Mean	0.9	0.9	0.8	0.7	0.8	0.6
Standard deviation	0.3	0.4	0.3	0.2	0.1	0.3

Daily minimum specific conductance (μS/cm)

Statistic	C3	C4	C5	C6	C7	C8
n	76	76	81	65	57	77
Minimum	127	129	106	191	162	142
P25	224	225	179	265	241	194
Median	294	296	241	300	272	273
P75	317	319	256	307	298	293
Maximum	358	366	288	333	330	349
Mean	267	268	219	284	262	248
Standard deviation	67	66	46	35	46	59

Daily mean specific conductance (μS/cm)

Statistic	C3	C4	C5	C6	C7	C8
n	76	76	80	65	57	77
Minimum	129	131	146	198	187	144
P25	229	237	197	281	263	199
Median	313	308	251	305	294	279
P75	326	327	265	313	306	298
Maximum	364	368	300	345	344	352
Mean	276	278	231	293	280	254
Standard deviation	69	67	44	33	37	60

Daily maximum specific conductance (μS/cm)

Statistic	C3	C4	C5	C6	C7	C8
n	76	76	81	65	57	77
Minimum	130	133	157	202	214	146
P25	240	248	199	298	276	205
Median	319	318	256	311	304	285
P75	336	334	272	320	314	303
Maximum	368	369	305	355	354	356
Mean	286	287	238	300	293	260
Standard deviation	68	67	45	34	31	61

Daily specific conductance range (μS/cm)

Statistic	C3	C4	C5	C6	C7	C8
n	76	76	80	65	57	77
Minimum	2	3	2	3	3	1
P25	11	10	7	7	12	7
Median	16	17	13	12	16	10
P75	24	23	18	18	50	15
Maximum	61	69	169	125	96	47
Mean	19	20	19	17	31	12
Standard deviation	12	13	26	20	26	8

Table 1–2. Summary statistics for water-quality data collected at selected stations in the Susquehanna River Basin, Pennsylvania, May 1 through July 31, 2009

[C3, Susquehanna River below Clemson Island (Main Channel); C4, Susquehanna River at Clemson Island (Microhabitat); C5, Juniata River at Newport; C8, Susquehanna River at Harrisburg; C, degrees Celsius; µS/cm, microsiemens per centimeter; mg/L, milligrams per liter; n, number of daily values; P25, 25th percentile; P75, 75th percentile]

Statistic	Daily minimum temperature (°C)				Daily mean temperature (°C)				Daily maximum temperature (°C)				Daily temperature range (°C)			
	C3	C4	C5	C8	C3	C4	C5	C8	C3	C4	C5	C8	C3	C4	C5	C8
n	86	86	91	87	86	86	91	87	86	86	91	87	86	86	91	87
Minimum	15.2	15.1	11.1	11.7	16.2	16.2	11.6	12.8	16.9	16.8	13.0	14.2	0.6	0.9	0.9	0.6
P25	18.0	17.8	15.8	17.9	19.2	19.2	16.9	18.6	20.5	20.3	17.8	19.7	2.2	2.2	1.8	1.6
Median	21.9	21.6	20.0	21.6	23.4	23.2	21.2	22.5	24.5	24.2	22.4	23.5	2.8	2.6	2.4	2.3
P75	23.1	22.7	21.4	23.6	24.6	24.3	23.1	24.8	26.2	26.1	24.4	26.0	3.3	3.4	3.3	2.7
Maximum	25.3	24.4	24.1	26.2	26.5	26.1	25.3	26.8	29.1	28.6	27.3	28.1	4.8	5.6	4.9	4.8
Mean	20.6	20.4	18.7	20.6	21.9	21.8	20.0	21.7	23.4	23.3	21.3	22.8	2.8	2.8	2.6	2.2
Standard deviation	2.9	2.7	3.4	3.5	3.0	2.9	3.6	3.6	3.3	3.2	3.9	3.7	1.0	1.1	1.0	0.8

Statistic	Daily minimum dissolved oxygen (mg/L)				Daily mean dissolved oxygen (mg/L)				Daily maximum dissolved oxygen (mg/L)				Daily dissolved oxygen range (mg/L)			
	C3	C4	C5	C8	C3	C4	C5	C8	C3	C4	C5	C8	C3	C4	C5	C8
n	86	86	92	87	86	86	92	87	86	86	92	87	86	86	92	87
Minimum	6.3	4.5	5.7	5.7	7.7	6.3	7.4	6.9	7.9	7.7	8.4	7.4	0.3	0.4	0.4	0.4
P25	7.1	6.1	6.9	6.6	8.6	7.7	8.5	7.9	10.2	9.1	9.9	9.0	2.0	1.8	1.7	1.6
Median	7.7	7.0	7.7	7.3	9.3	8.3	9.2	8.5	11.0	10.2	10.6	9.9	2.9	3.1	2.7	2.3
P75	8.8	8.2	8.6	8.5	10.0	9.2	9.7	9.4	11.6	10.7	11.9	10.4	4.1	4.1	4.4	2.7
Maximum	9.5	9.4	9.7	10.1	10.8	10.2	10.4	10.5	13.2	12.6	13.8	11.3	5.7	6.2	7.7	3.8
Mean	7.9	7.0	7.7	7.5	9.3	8.4	9.1	8.6	10.9	10.0	10.8	9.7	3.0	3.0	3.1	2.2
Standard deviation	0.9	1.2	1.1	1.1	0.8	0.9	0.7	0.9	1.2	1.1	1.3	0.9	1.4	1.4	1.9	0.9

Table 1–2.   Summary statistics for water-quality data collected at selected stations in the Susquehanna River Basin, Pennsylvania, May 1 through July 31, 2009.—Continued

[C3, Susquehanna River below Clemson Island (Main Channel); C4, Susquehanna River at Clemson Island (Microhabitat); C5, Juniata River at Newport; C8, Susquehanna River at Harrisburg;   C, degrees Celsius; µS/cm, microsiemens per centimeter; mg/L, milligrams per liter; n, number of daily values; P25, 25th percentile; P75, 75th percentile]

Statistic	Daily minimum pH (standard units)				Daily median pH (standard units)				Daily maximum pH (standard units)				Daily pH range (standard units)			
	Station				Station				Station				Station			
	C3	C4	C5	C8	C3	C4	C5	C8	C3	C4	C5	C8	C3	C4	C5	C8
n	86	86	92	87	86	86	92	87	86	86	92	87	86	86	92	87
Minimum	7.3	7.2	6.8	7.2	7.4	7.4	6.9	7.4	7.5	7.5	7.2	7.5	0.1	0.1	0.0	0.1
P25	7.6	7.4	7.5	7.4	8.1	7.7	7.6	7.7	8.5	8.2	8.0	8.1	0.8	0.6	0.5	0.5
Median	7.8	7.6	7.6	7.6	8.3	7.9	7.8	8.0	8.8	8.5	8.3	8.5	0.9	0.9	0.7	0.8
P75	7.9	7.7	7.7	7.7	8.6	8.2	8.1	8.3	9.0	8.7	8.7	8.8	1.1	1.2	1.0	1.1
Maximum	8.6	8.0	8.1	8.3	9.1	8.8	8.7	8.8	9.4	9.1	9.0	9.1	1.5	1.6	1.3	1.4
Mean	7.8	7.5	7.6	7.6	8.3	8.0	7.9	8.0	8.8	8.4	8.3	8.4	0.9	0.9	0.7	0.8
Standard deviation	0.3	0.2	0.2	0.2	0.4	0.3	0.4	0.4	0.4	0.4	0.5	0.4	0.3	0.4	0.3	0.3

Statistic	Daily minimum specific conductance (µS/cm)				Daily mean specific conductance (µS/cm)				Daily maximum specific conductance (µS/cm)				Daily specific conductance range (µS/cm)			
	Station				Station				Station				Station			
	C3	C4	C5	C8	C3	C4	C5	C8	C3	C4	C5	C8	C3	C4	C5	C8
n	86	86	92	87	86	86	92	87	86	86	92	87	86	86	92	87
Minimum	146	165	120	149	157	170	131	162	165	173	143	165	3	4	3	2
P25	184	192	171	182	192	204	177	185	201	216	183	190	8	11	8	5
Median	202	208	196	195	209	218	205	198	215	233	213	208	14	19	11	10
P75	227	235	230	221	235	248	245	221	244	254	252	233	21	28	17	17
Maximum	277	274	276	259	285	282	279	266	297	289	293	277	46	53	116	65
Mean	207	214	198	200	215	224	210	206	222	234	217	213	15	20	19	12
Standard deviation	32	30	37	28	33	29	38	29	34	29	39	29	9	11	21	10

Table 1–3. Summary statistics for water-quality data collected at selected sampling stations in the Susquehanna River Basin, Pennsylvania, May 1 through July 31, 2010.

[C5, Juniata River at Newport ; C6, Juniata River near Howe Township Park (Microhabitat); C8, Susquehanna River at Harrisburg; C, degrees Celsius; µS/cm, microsiemens per centimeter; mg/L, milligrams per liter; n, number of daily values; P25, 25th percentile; P75, 75th percentile]

Statistic	Daily minimum temperature (°C) Station			Daily mean temperature (°C) Station			Daily maximum temperature (°C) Station			Daily temperature range (°C) Station		
	C5	C6	C8	C5	C6	C8	C5	C6	C8	C5	C6	C8
n	86	88	84	86	88	84	86	88	84	86	88	84
Minimum	11.3	12.0	12.4	11.5	12.3	13.0	11.9	12.5	13.5	0.6	0.4	1.0
P25	18.7	18.9	21.6	20.0	20.1	23.3	21.6	21.5	25.0	2.1	2.0	2.2
Median	22.7	23.4	25.3	24.2	24.5	26.5	25.7	26.1	27.8	2.8	2.7	2.9
P75	25.4	26.1	27.3	27.1	27.8	28.9	28.9	29.3	30.4	4.0	3.4	3.5
Maximum	27.9	28.7	29.7	30.1	30.8	31.4	32.5	33.2	33.4	6.0	6.7	4.5
Mean	21.8	22.3	23.7	23.3	23.7	25.1	24.7	25.0	26.5	3.0	2.8	2.8
Standard deviation	4.4	4.6	4.8	4.8	4.9	4.9	5.1	5.1	5.1	1.3	1.2	0.9

Statistic	Daily minimum dissolved oxygen (mg/L) Station			Daily mean dissolved oxygen (mg/L) Station			Daily maximum dissolved oxygen (mg/L) Station			Daily dissolved oxygen range (mg/L) Station		
	C5	C6	C8	C5	C6	C8	C5	C6	C8	C5	C6	C8
n	87	88	85	87	88	85	87	88	85	87	88	85
Minimum	4.1	3.5	4.1	6.3	5.7	5.8	7.1	7.4	6.9	0.1	0.4	0.4
P25	5.6	5.4	5.2	7.8	7.5	7.0	9.5	9.0	8.8	1.9	1.9	2.1
Median	6.6	6.1	5.8	8.4	8.1	7.6	10.5	10.0	9.4	3.2	3.1	2.9
P75	7.9	7.3	7.1	8.8	8.9	8.2	11.5	10.9	10.1	5.5	5.2	4.1
Maximum	10.0	10.0	10.0	10.9	10.6	10.7	12.5	13.2	11.3	7.5	8.0	6.2
Mean	6.7	6.4	6.4	8.4	8.2	7.8	10.4	10.0	9.4	3.6	3.6	3.1

Table 1–3.   Summary statistics for water-quality data collected at selected sampling stations in the Susquehanna River Basin, Pennsylvania, May 1 through July 31, 2010. —Continued

[C5, Juniata River at Newport ; C6, Juniata River near Howe Township Park (Microhabitat); C8, Susquehanna River at Harrisburg; C, degrees Celsius; µS/cm, microsiemens per centimeter; mg/L, milligrams per liter; n, number of daily values; P25, 25th percentile; P75, 75th percentile]

Standard deviation	1.4	1.6	1.6	0.9	1.1	1.1	1.2	1.4	0.9	2.0	2.0	1.5

Statistic	Daily Minimum pH (standard units)			Daily Median pH (standard units)			Daily Maximum pH (standard units)			Daily pH Range (standard units)		
	Station			Station			Station			Station		
	C5	C6	C8	C5	C6	C8	C5	C6	C8	C5	C6	C8
n	87	88	85	87	88	85	87	88	85	87	88	85
Minimum	7.2	6.9	7.2	7.3	7.2	7.4	7.5	7.4	7.6	0.1	0.1	0.0
P25	7.6	7.5	7.4	7.8	7.8	7.6	8.2	8.1	8.0	0.6	0.5	0.5
Median	7.7	7.8	7.5	8.0	8.0	7.8	8.5	8.4	8.3	0.9	0.6	0.9
P75	7.8	8.0	7.6	8.4	8.4	8.1	8.8	8.7	8.6	1.0	0.7	1.1
Maximum	8.1	8.5	7.7	8.8	8.9	8.4	9.1	9.2	9.1	1.3	1.4	1.6
Mean	7.7	7.8	7.5	8.1	8.1	7.8	8.5	8.4	8.3	0.8	0.6	0.8
Standard deviation	0.2	0.3	0.1	0.3	0.4	0.3	0.4	0.4	0.4	0.3	0.2	0.4

Statistic	Daily minimum specific conductance (µS/cm)			Daily mean specific conductance (µS/cm)			Daily maximum specific conductance (µS/cm)			Daily specific conductance range (µS/cm)		
	Station			Station			Station			Station		
	C5	C6	C8	C5	C6	C8	C5	C6	C8	C5	C6	C8
n	87	88	85	87	88	85	87	88	85	87	88	85
Minimum	138	121	131	154	175	138	157	191	141	3	4	2
P25	189	211	192	196	221	196	202	231	199	8	10	7
Median	221	248	237	228	259	243	237	271	251	10	16	10
P75	260	287	287	270	296	298	277	307	300	14	23	16
Maximum	288	318	340	294	325	349	302	342	358	152	186	58
Mean	221	248	237	230	259	244	238	270	250	16	22	13
Standard deviation	40	43	59	39	41	59	39	41	59	23	25	9

Appendix 2.   Summary Statistics for Water-Quality Data Collected in the Delaware and Allegheny River Basins

Table 2–1.   Summary statistics for water-quality data collected at selected sampling stations in the Delaware and Allegheny River Basins, May 1 through July 31, 2008.

[C1, Delaware River at Trenton, N.J.; C10, Allegheny River at Lock and Dam 3 at Acmetonia, Pa.;   C, degrees Celsius; µS/cm, microsiemens per centimeter; mg/L, milligrams per liter; n, number of daily values; P25, 25th percentile; P75, 75th percentile]

Statistic	Daily minimum temperature (°C) Station		Daily mean temperature (°C) Station		Daily maximum temperature (°C) Station		Daily temperature range (°C) Station	
	C1	C10	C1	C10	C1	C10	C1	C10
n	87	92	87	92	87	92	87	92
Minimum	12.8	12.0	13.9	12.3	14.3	12.6	0.6	0.1
P25	18.0	15.0	18.8	15.2	19.9	15.6	1.6	0.7
Median	23.4	23.5	24.5	23.9	25.5	24.4	2.0	1.0
P75	25.5	24.9	26.7	25.4	27.9	26.4	2.5	1.5
Maximum	28.1	27.1	29.2	27.7	30.5	29.5	3.4	3.3
Mean	21.8	20.8	22.8	21.2	23.8	22.0	2.0	1.1
Standard deviation	4.7	5.1	4.8	5.2	5.0	5.5	0.7	0.6

Statistic	Daily minimum dissolved oxygen (mg/L) Station		Daily mean dissolved oxygen (mg/L) Station		Daily maximum dissolved oxygen (mg/L) Station		Daily dissolved oxygen range (mg/L) Station	
	C1	C10	C1	C10	C1	C10	C1	C10
n	87	85	87	85	87	85	87	85
Minimum	5.7	5.6	6.6	6.4	7.0	6.8	0.5	0.1
P25	7.4	6.6	8.9	7.0	9.9	7.3	1.3	0.3
Median	7.8	7.1	9.3	7.3	10.7	7.7	2.4	0.4
P75	8.8	9.0	9.7	9.1	11.2	9.3	3.4	0.6
Maximum	10.0	9.6	11.0	9.7	12.7	9.8	5.1	2.1
Mean	8.0	7.6	9.2	7.9	10.4	8.1	2.4	0.5
Standard deviation	1.1	1.2	1.0	1.1	1.3	1.0	1.3	0.4

Table 2–1. Summary statistics for water-quality data collected at selected sampling stations in the Delaware and Allegheny River Basins, May 1 through July 31, 2008.—Continued

[C1, Delaware River at Trenton, N.J.; C10, Allegheny River at Lock and Dam 3 at Acmetonia, Pa.; C, degrees Celsius; µS/cm, microsiemens per centimeter; mg/L, milligrams per liter; n, number of daily values; P25, 25th percentile; P75, 75th percentile]

Statistic	Daily minimum pH (standard units) Station		Daily median pH (standard units) Station		Daily maximum pH (standard units) Station		Daily pH range (standard units) Station	
	C1	C10	C1	C10	C1	C10	C1	C10
n	87	91	87	91	87	91	87	91
Minimum	7.1	6.6	7.2	6.7	7.2	6.7	0.1	0.0
P25	7.8	6.7	8.0	6.8	8.3	6.8	0.5	0.1
Median	8.0	6.9	8.4	7.0	8.8	7.0	0.7	0.1
P75	8.2	7.3	8.8	7.4	9.1	7.4	0.8	0.2
Maximum	8.8	7.5	9.2	7.6	9.4	7.7	1.1	0.4
Mean	8.0	7.0	8.4	7.1	8.7	7.1	0.6	0.1
Standard deviation	0.4	0.3	0.5	0.3	0.6	0.3	0.3	0.1

Statistic	Daily minimum specific conductance (µS/cm) Station		Daily mean specific conductance (µS/cm) Station		Daily maximum specific conductance (µS/cm) Station		Daily specific conductance range (µS/cm) Station	
	C1	C10	C1	C10	C1	C10	C1	C10
n	87	92	87	92	87	92	87	92
Minimum	105	214	110	220	118	224	2	2
P25	198	241	204	248	209	255	5	8
Median	217	264	222	271	227	283	7	11
P75	234	296	239	301	245	306	11	16
Maximum	254	361	261	367	266	375	123	64
Mean	212	269	218	276	223	283	11	14
Standard deviation	32	35	30	36	29	38	14	11

Table 2-2. Summary statistics for water-quality data collected at selected sampling stations in the Delaware and Allegheny River Basins, May 1 through July 31, 2009.

[C1, Delaware River at Trenton, N.J.; C10, Allegheny River at Lock and Dam 3 at Acmetonia, Pa.; C, degrees Celsius; µS/cm, microsiemens per centimeter; mg/L, milligrams per liter; n, number of daily values; P25, 25th percentile; P75, 75th percentile]

Statistic	Daily minimum temperature (°C) Station		Daily mean temperature (°C) Station		Daily maximum temperature (°C) Station		Daily temperature range (°C) Station	
	C1	C10	C1	C10	C1	C10	C1	C10
n	91	92	91	92	91	92	91	92
Minimum	14.6	14.5	14.9	14.8	15.6	14.9	0.3	0.3
P25	17.4	18.0	17.9	18.3	18.5	18.6	1.0	0.4
Median	19.4	21.4	20.0	21.7	20.8	22.3	1.4	0.7
P75	21.8	23.1	22.5	23.4	23.2	23.9	1.7	1.2
Maximum	25.0	24.1	25.8	24.7	27.0	25.9	2.9	2.4
Mean	19.6	20.4	20.2	20.7	21.0	21.3	1.4	0.9
Standard deviation	2.8	3.0	2.9	3.1	3.0	3.3	0.5	0.5

Statistic	Daily minimum dissolved oxygen (mg/L) Station		Daily mean dissolved oxygen (mg/L) Station		Daily maximum dissolved oxygen (mg/L) Station		Daily dissolved oxygen range (mg/L) Station	
	C1	C10	C1	C10	C1	C10	C1	C10
n	91	84	91	84	91	84	91	84
Minimum	6.8	6.4	7.4	6.9	7.8	7.1	0.1	0.1
P25	8.4	7.2	8.8	7.3	9.2	7.5	0.5	0.2
Median	8.7	7.6	9.2	7.8	9.6	8.0	0.7	0.3
P75	9.0	8.8	9.5	9.0	10.1	9.2	1.7	0.4
Maximum	9.6	9.4	10.2	9.5	12.8	9.6	4.8	0.9
Mean	8.6	7.9	9.2	8.1	9.8	8.2	1.2	0.4
Standard deviation	0.6	0.9	0.6	0.8	0.9	0.8	1.1	0.2

Table 2–2. Summary statistics for water-quality data collected at selected sampling stations in the Delaware and Allegheny River Basins, May 1 through July 31, 2009.—Continued

[C1, Delaware River at Trenton, N.J.; C10, Allegheny River at Lock and Dam 3 at Acmetonia, Pa.; C, degrees Celsius; μS/cm, microsiemens per centimeter; mg/L, milligrams per liter; n, number of daily values; P25, 25th percentile; P75, 75th percentile]

Statistic	Daily minimum pH (standard units)		Daily median pH (standard units)		Daily maximum pH (standard units)		Daily pH range (standard units)	
	Station		Station		Station		Station	
	C1	C10	C1	C10	C1	C10	C1	C10
n	91	92	91	92	91	92	91	92
Minimum	7.1	7.0	7.3	7.1	7.4	7.1	0.1	0.0
P25	7.5	7.2	7.6	7.3	7.7	7.3	0.2	0.0
Median	7.6	7.3	7.7	7.3	7.8	7.4	0.3	0.1
P75	7.7	7.3	8.0	7.4	8.4	7.4	0.5	0.1
Maximum	8.8	7.5	9.1	7.5	9.3	7.6	1.3	0.3
Mean	7.7	7.3	7.8	7.3	8.0	7.4	0.4	0.1
Standard deviation	0.4	0.1	0.4	0.1	0.5	0.1	0.2	0.1

Statistic	Daily minimum specific conductance (μS/cm)		Daily mean specific conductance (μS/cm)		Daily maximum specific conductance (μS/cm)		Daily specific conductance range (μS/cm)	
	Station		Station		Station		Station	
	C1	C10	C1	C10	C1	C10	C1	C10
n	91	92	91	92	91	92	91	92
Minimum	120	194	122	197	123	199	3	2
P25	152	239	162	246	168	252	6	6
Median	175	249	185	255	190	264	9	13
P75	202	264	207	268	215	276	13	21
Maximum	224	298	231	306	248	312	82	50
Mean	176	249	182	256	189	264	13	14
Standard deviation	31	22	30	23	31	24	13	10

Table 2–3. Summary statistics for water-quality data collected at selected sampling stations on the Delaware and Allegheny River Basins, May 1 through July 31, 2010.

[C1, Delaware River at Trenton, N.J.; C10, Allegheny River at Lock and Dam 3 at Acmetonia, Pa.; C, degrees Celsius; µS/cm, microsiemens per centimeter; mg/L, milligrams per liter; n, number of daily values; P25, 25th percentile; P75, 75th percentile]

Statistic	Daily minimum temperature (°C)		Daily mean temperature (°C)		Daily maximum temperature (°C)		Daily temperature range (°C)	
	Station		Station		Station		Station	
	C1	C10	C1	C10	C1	C10	C1	C10
n	80	92	80	92	80	92	80	92
Minimum	12.3	12.4	13.4	12.7	14.0	13.0	0.4	0.2
P25	19.5	17.8	20.3	18.0	21.3	18.3	1.7	0.6
Median	23.9	23.5	25.1	23.9	26.2	24.4	2.2	0.8
P75	26.4	27.2	27.6	27.5	28.9	27.9	2.6	1.1
Maximum	28.7	28.5	29.7	28.7	30.9	29.5	3.8	1.9
Mean	22.8	22.2	23.8	22.6	24.9	23.1	2.1	0.9
Standard deviation	4.6	5.1	4.7	5.1	4.9	5.1	0.7	0.4

Statistic	Daily minimum dissolved oxygen (mg/L)		Daily mean dissolved oxygen (mg/L)		Daily maximum dissolved oxygen (mg/L)		Daily dissolved oxygen range (mg/L)	
	Station		Station		Station		Station	
	C1	C10	C1	C10	C1	C10	C1	C10
n	80	92	80	92	80	92	80	92
Minimum	6.3	5.0	7.1	5.5	7.7	6.0	0.5	0.1
P25	7.2	6.2	8.6	6.7	9.6	7.1	1.4	0.2
Median	7.8	7.1	9.3	7.2	10.4	7.6	2.1	0.4
P75	8.7	8.9	9.9	9.0	11.4	9.1	3.0	0.8
Maximum	10.6	10.5	11.7	10.6	15.7	10.7	7.9	1.7
Mean	8.0	7.4	9.3	7.7	10.7	8.0	2.7	0.6
Standard deviation	1.0	1.5	1.0	1.3	1.8	1.2	1.9	0.4

Table 2–3. Summary statistics for water-quality data collected at selected sampling stations on the Delaware and Allegheny River Basins, May 1 through July 31, 2010.—Continued

[C1, Delaware River at Trenton, N.J.; C10, Allegheny River at Lock and Dam 3 at Acmetonia, Pa.; C, degrees Celsius; µS/cm, microsiemens per centimeter; mg/L, milligrams per liter; n, number of daily values; P25, 25th percentile; P75, 75th percentile]

Statistic	Daily minimum pH (standard units)		Daily median pH (standard units)		Daily maximum pH (standard units)		Daily pH range (standard units)	
	Station		Station		Station		Station	
	C1	C10	C1	C10	C1	C10	C1	C10
n	80	92	80	92	80	92	80	92
Minimum	7.3	7.0	7.5	7.2	7.7	7.2	0.1	0.0
P25	7.6	7.2	7.7	7.2	7.9	7.3	0.4	0.0
Median	7.7	7.2	8.0	7.3	8.4	7.4	0.6	0.1
P75	8.0	7.3	8.6	7.4	8.9	7.4	0.8	0.1
Maximum	8.5	7.5	9.1	7.5	9.4	7.6	1.2	0.4
Mean	7.8	7.3	8.1	7.3	8.4	7.4	0.6	0.1
Standard deviation	0.3	0.1	0.5	0.1	0.5	0.1	0.3	0.1

Statistic	Daily minimum specific conductance (µS/cm)		Daily mean specific conductance (µS/cm)		Daily maximum specific conductance (µS/cm)		Daily specific conductance range (µS/cm)	
	Station		Station		Station		Station	
	C1	C10	C1	C10	C1	C10	C1	C10
n	80	92	80	92	80	92	80	92
Minimum	165	170	170	173	181	176	3	1
P25	212	234	217	237	222	246	6	7
Median	234	254	241	261	243	265	8	11
P75	245	335	250	340	254	346	11	20
Maximum	272	435	276	465	277	482	45	60
Mean	230	281	235	289	239	296	10	15
Standard deviation	23	69	23	71	23	73	6	11

For additional information:
Director
U.S. Geological Survey
215 Limekiln Road
New Cumberland, PA 17070

http://pa.water.usgs.gov/

Document prepared by the West Trenton Publishing Service Center